Contents

Foreword
by Stoo Cambridge

Whenever you see 'C64' mentioned anywhere what do you think? Do you hear the insanely good Rambo loading music, which as a kid I often reloaded just to listen to it again? Or perhaps the technically stunning Mayhem in Monsterland that brought console-like gaming to our beloved 8-bit wonder? Oh and what about the Rob Hubbard Compunet Thrust Concert demo created by Stoat and Tim? I recall buying Thrust after seeing Rob's credits on the box (come on who didn't do that?), luckily it was a great buy and turned out to be one of my all time faves! I could also mention the surrealist Wizball, a game I sat, played and managed to complete over a whole weekend! Much to my parents' complete bewilderment when I was letting out jubilant cheers from my bedroom, I have to add.

There are so many magical C64 moments I could mention but I guess the fact that a machine born in the early '80s is still so fondly remembered and talked about today, well that in itself speaks volumes. These were some of my C64 memories, what are yours? Viva C64 forever!

Stoo Cambridge, graphic artist
June 2014

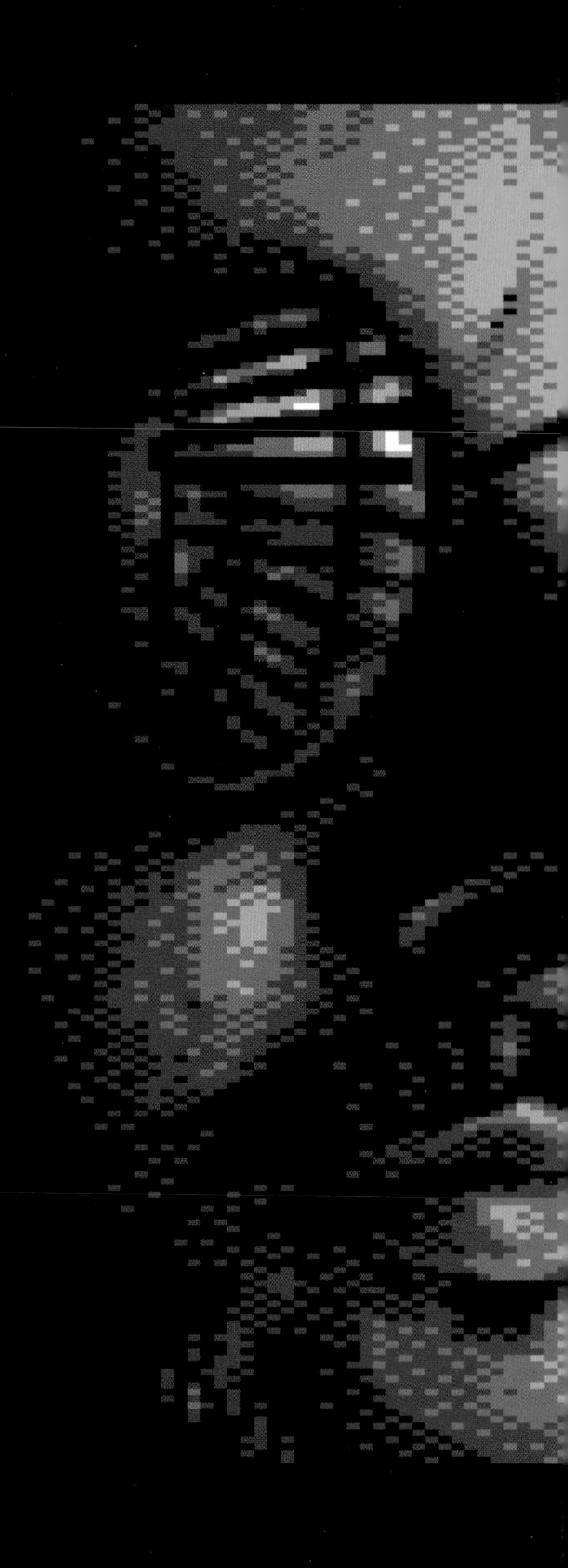

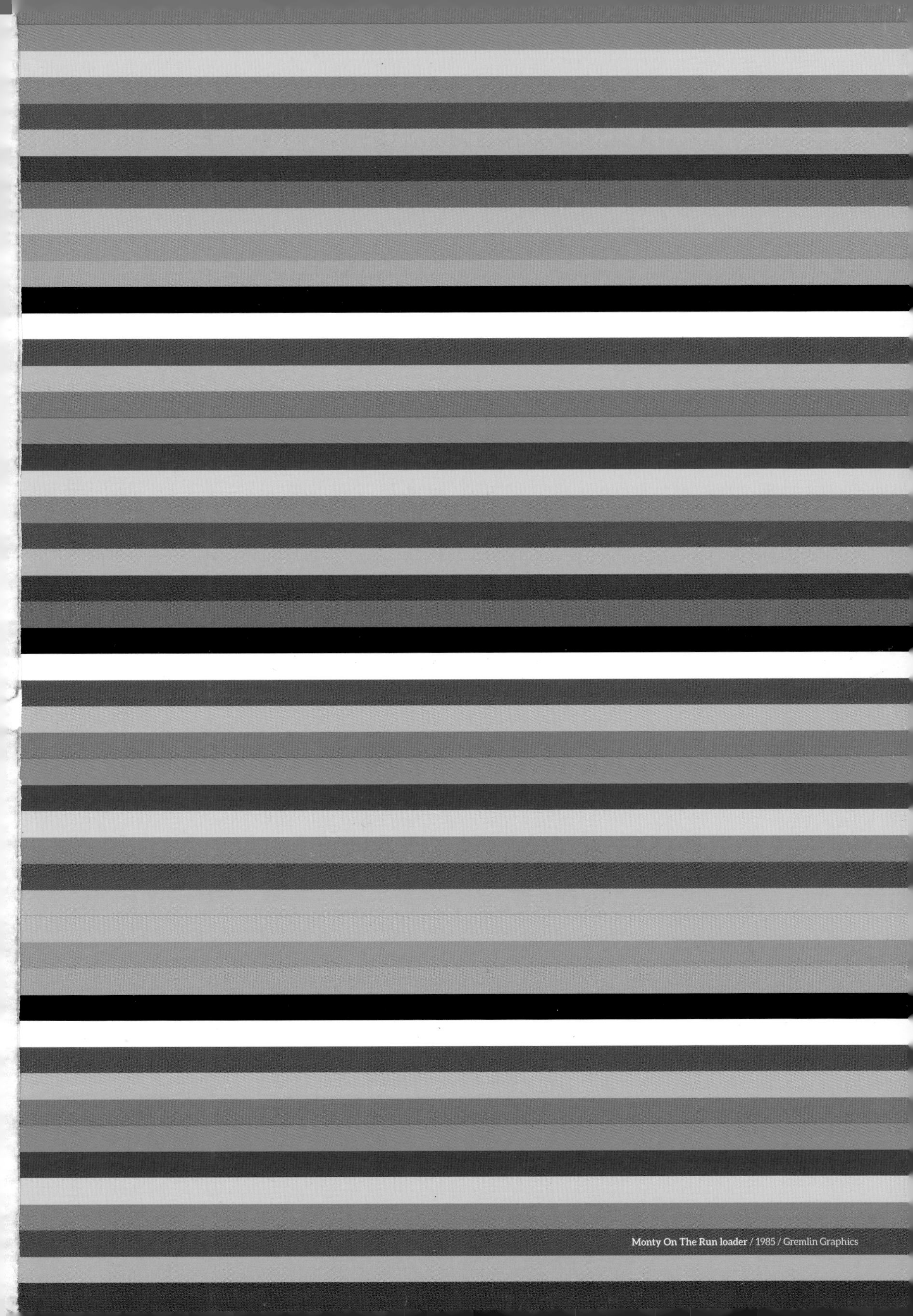

Monty On The Run loader / 1985 / Gremlin Graphics

A huge thanks to all contributors to this book

Mat Allen
C64 fan and collector

Steve Brown
Game designer

Stoo Cambridge
Graphic artist

Gary Carr
Graphic artist

David Crane
Game designer and programmer

Karen Davies-Downey
Graphic artist and co-founder of Denton Designs

Steven Day (STE'86)
Graphic artist

Mevlut Dinc
Programmer and founder of Vivid Image

Paul Docherty (DOKK)
Graphic artist

Andy Dyer
Ex-Commodore Format reviewer

Oliver Frey
Artist

Kevin Furry
Game designer and programmer

Ron Gilbert
Game designer and programmer

Jon Hare
Game designer, graphic artist and founder of Sensible Software

Andrew Hewson
Founder of Hewson Consultants

Robin Hogg
Ex-Zzap!64 reviewer

Steve Jarratt
Ex-Zzap!64 deputy editor and editor of Commodore Format

Roger Kean
Founder of Newsfield

Phil King
Ex-Zzap!64 reviewer

Paul Koller
Games programmer

John F. Kutcher
Game designer and programmer

James Leach
Ex-Commodore Format reviewer

Robin Levy
Game designer and graphic artist

Peter Liepa
Game designer and programmer

Oliver Lindau
Graphic artist

Steinar Lund
Illustrator

Michal Okowicki
Games programmer

*Archer MacLean**
Game designer and programmer

Jordan Mechner
Game designer and programmer

*Alan Miller***
Founder of Accolade

Jeff Minter
Game designer and programmer

Paul Norman
Game designer and programmer

Philip Oliver
Game designer and programmer

Gary Penn
Ex-Zzap!64 editor and reviewer

Jason Perkins
Game designer, programmer and graphic artist

Simon Phipps
Game designer, programmer and graphic artist

Jacco Van 't Riet
Graphic artist

Hugh Riley
Graphic artist

Andy Roberts
Game designer and programmer

Stephen Robertson (SIR)
Graphic artist

John Rowlands
Game designer and programmer

*Stephen Ruddy****
Game designer and programmer

Mat Sneap
Graphic artist

Bob Stevenson
Game designer and graphic artist

Jonathan Smyth Temples
Game designer and graphic artist

Stephen Ian Thomson (S.I.T)
Graphic artist

Martin Walker
Game designer, musician and programmer

Matt Wilsher
Photography

Stuart Wynne
Ex-Zzap!64 editor and reviewer

Guest reviewers
Luca Argentiero
Marc Bell
Jerry Bonner
Rocco Di Leo
Sam Dyer
GamesYouLoved
Andy Hayes
Dave Perry
Christian A. Schiller
Zack Scott
John Stanley
Andreas Wanda

*Archer MacLean quote courtesy of www.dadgum.com / **Alan Miller quote courtesy of www.theguardian.com/uk / ***Stephen Ruddy quote courtesy of Frank Gasking and www.C64.com

SIT

“It’s time to create computers for the masses, not the classes.”

Jack Tramiel, Founder, Commodore International

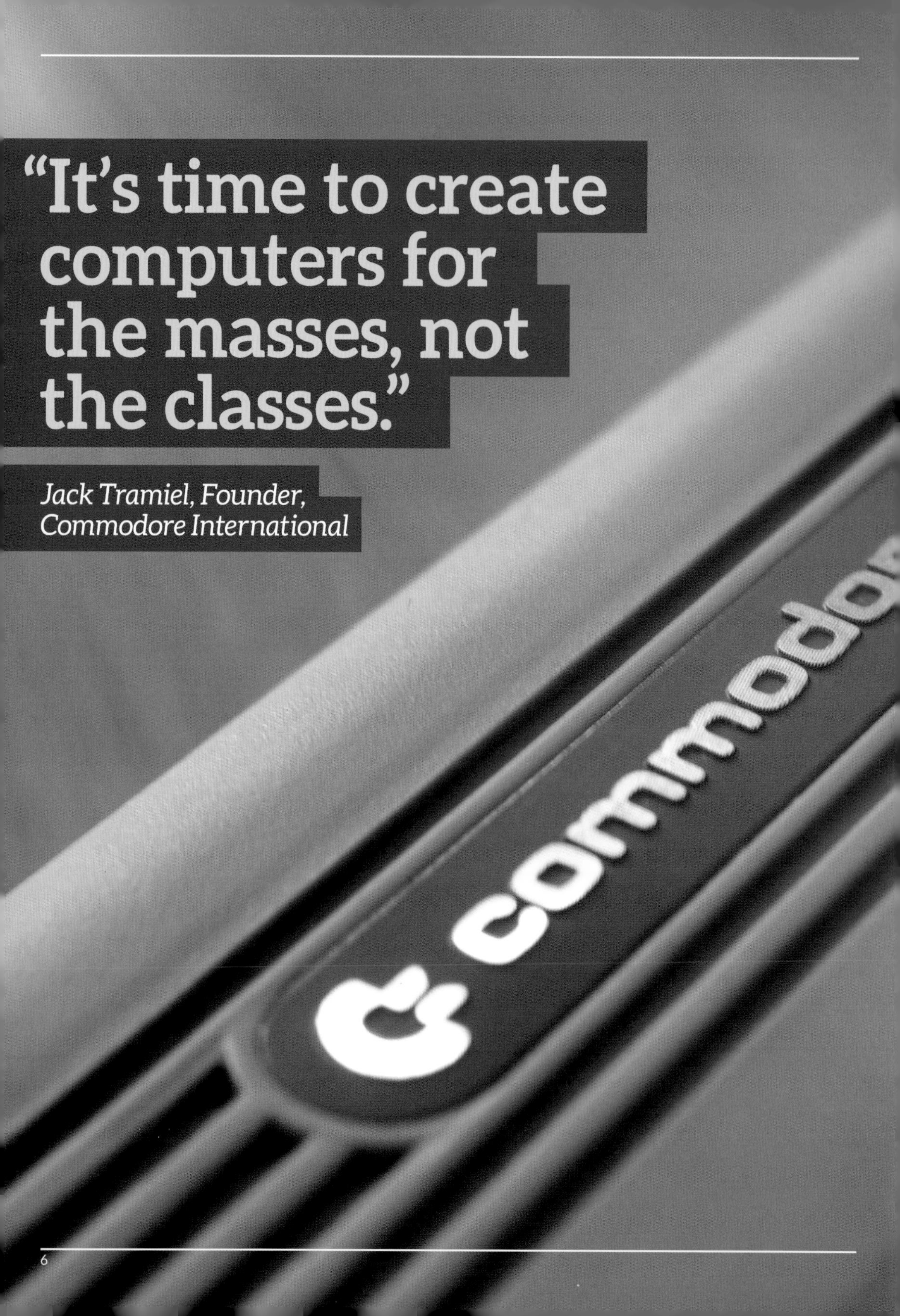

Jupiter Lander

"I remember playing this as a youngster because it came bundled in with my hand-me-down C64. Looking back now, it had terribly primitive graphics, simplistic gameplay and was clearly a rip-off of Atari's Lunar Lander. The aim of the game was to manoeuvre your module onto the various landing pads whilst using the least amount of thrust possible. The less thrust you used, the more points you got, simple. Probably most famous for being credited as the first game ever released for the Commodore 64."

Sam Dyer

x5

Released
1982

Genre
Arcade

Developer
HAL Laboratory

Publisher
Commodore

x2

x10

Beach-Head

"When I first saw Beach-Head featured on Dutch television back in 1985, it was actually my dad who said 'We need to get this!' We had the greatest time playing it together, especially the artillery shootout where he would call out the distances and I would do elevation adjustments and fire. The pace of the game and its pressure to take out the enemy quickly were really good, as were the graphics and sound. A true classic."

Martijn Bosschaart

Released
1983

Genre
Shooter

Developer
Access Software

Publisher
U.S. Gold

Blue Max

"This is one of those games that really takes me back to a great place and time. To this day, whenever I hear Rule, Britannia! I still think of Blue Max. The game just had so much going on, and seemed so wide open for the time. It was akin to Zaxxon but it was deeper. It was one of the few games that was well worth the 15 minutes it took the damn tape to load!"

Jerry Bonner

Released
1983

Genre
Scrolling shooter

Developer
Synapse Software

Publisher
U.S. Gold

Attack of the Mutant Camels

"The idea for Attack of the Mutant Camels came from seeing a review of The Empire Strikes Back game where the Walkers were described as 'giant mechanical camels'. I thought 'why not!?' I was given a US C64 and one of the first things I did with it was write a sprite editor in BASIC and used it to make the giant camel sprites. On a PAL machine sometimes the camels' bums fall off due to a timing issue. You can tell it's an early game due to the lack of raster scroll."

Released
1983

Genre
Scrolling shooter

Developer
Jeff Minter

Publisher
Llamasoft

International Soccer

"I'll always have a soft spot for International Soccer as it was the first game I ever played on my beloved C64. I spent hours upon hours as a child creating my own horrendously coloured kits (a neat feature), running the full length of the pitch with the ball stuck to my head and listening to that unforgettable 'phud' noise when you kicked the ball. The iconic image of the two huge player sprites before the game will stay with me forever."

Sam Dyer

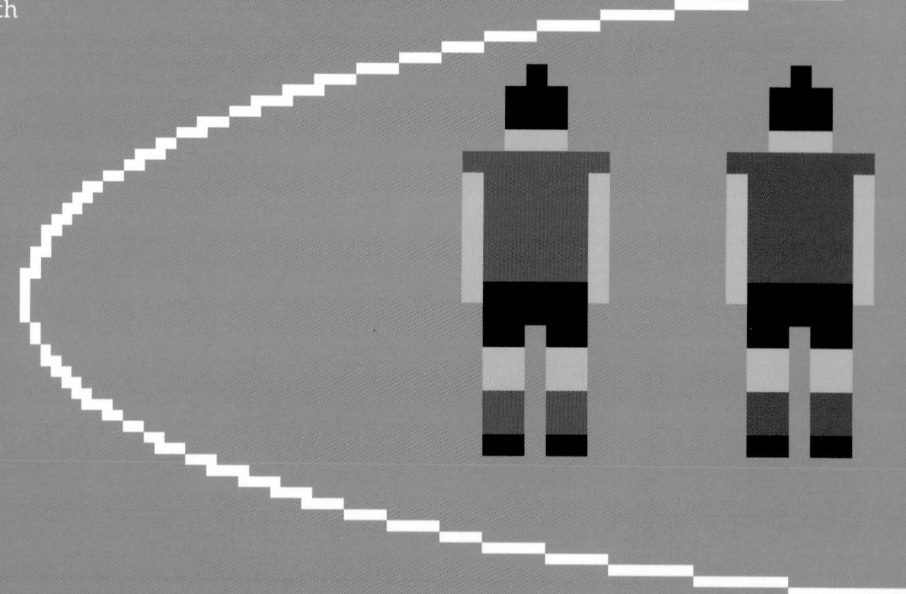

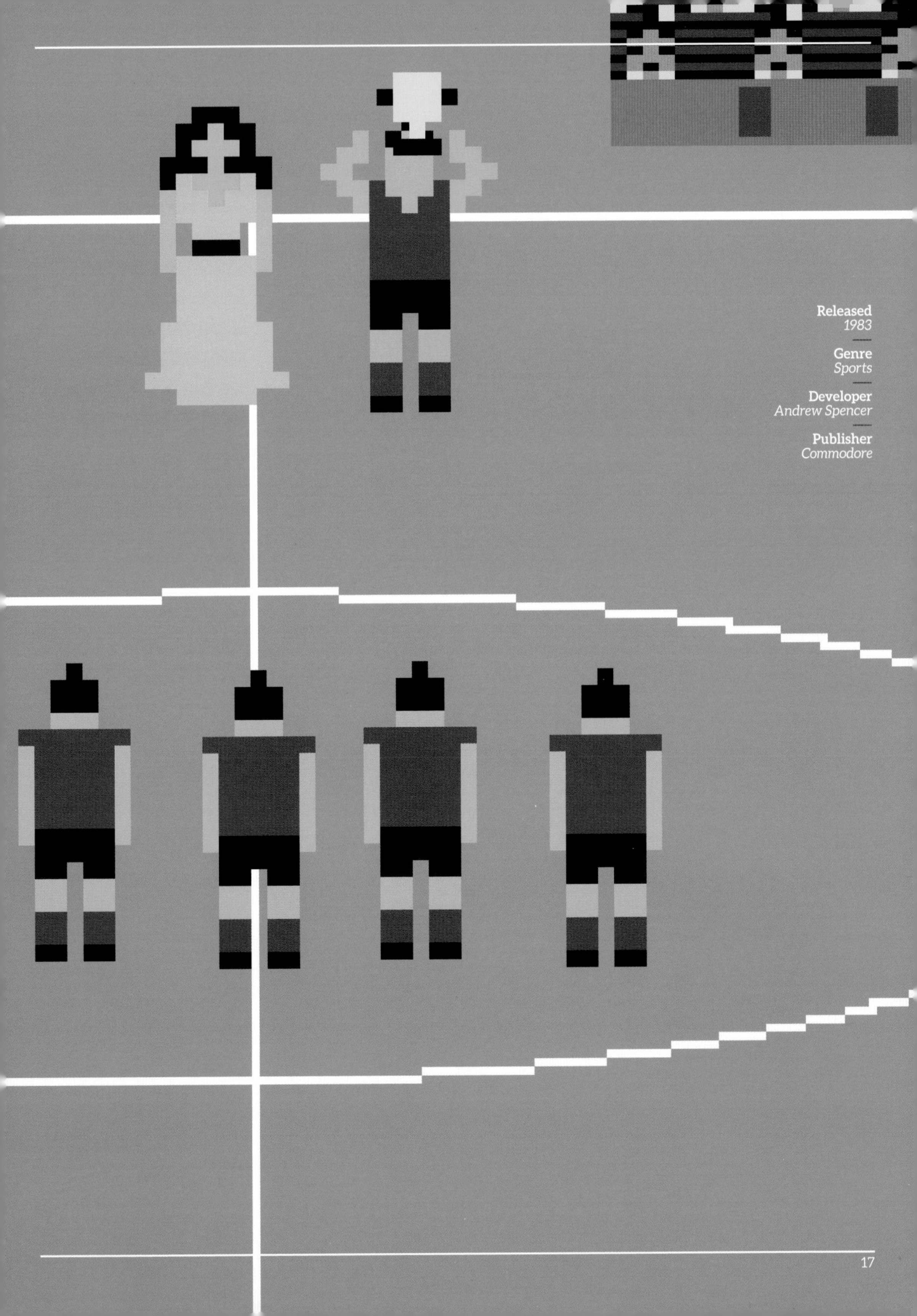

Released
1983

Genre
Sports

Developer
Andrew Spencer

Publisher
Commodore

Released
1983

Genre
Action

Developer
COSMI

Publisher
U.S. Gold

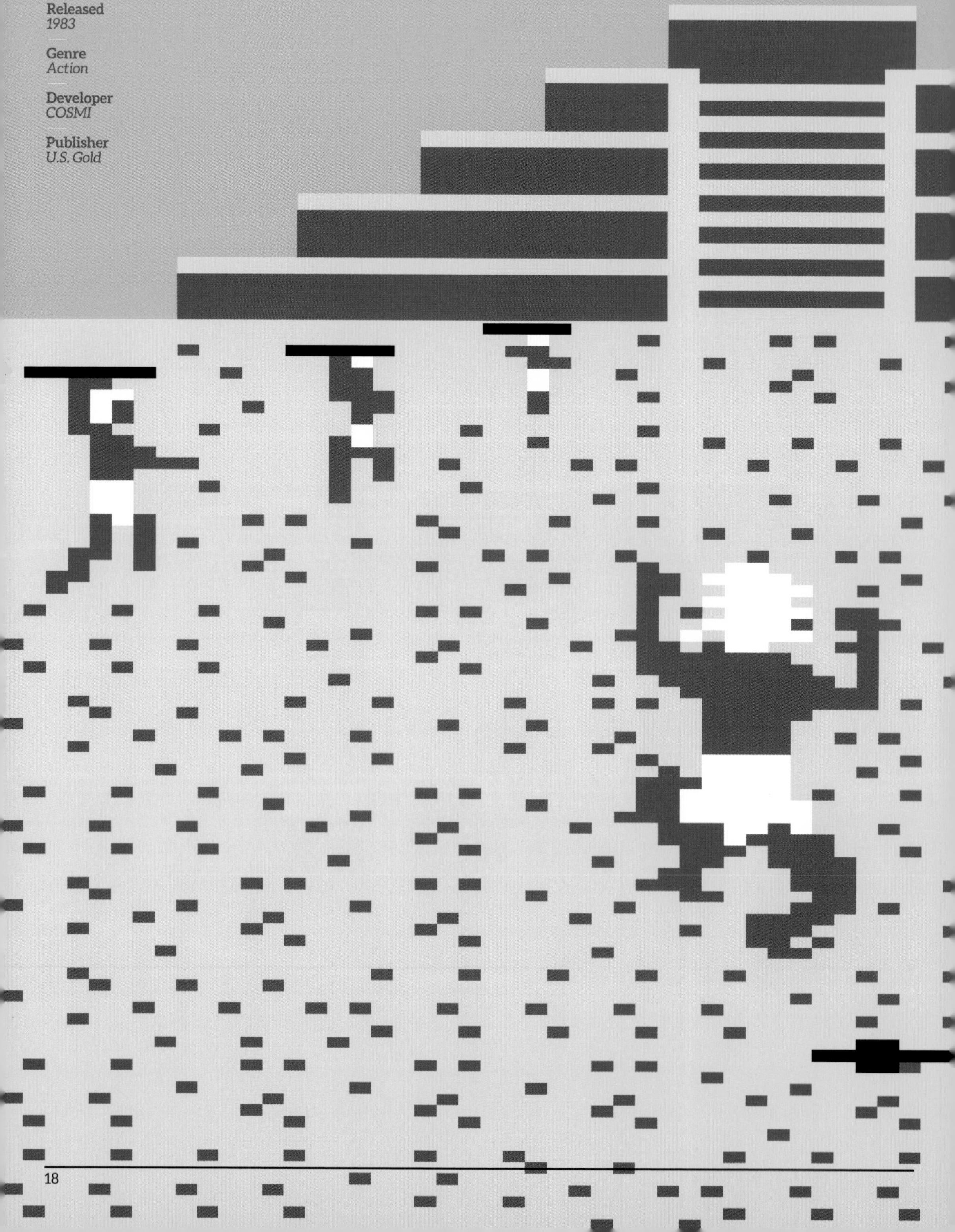

"Aztec Challenge was originally created by another COSMI programmer in the style of Mario Bros before my arrival. I was asked if I could do a port to the C64 and for one reason or another I went off and made a completely new game from scratch that in no way resembled the first except for the title."

Paul Norman

Lode Runner

Originally developed as a monochromatic game with ASCII artwork, programmer Douglas E. Smith took out a loan to buy a colour monitor for a more commercial version that got him signed to Brøderbund. It was comparable to Boulder Dash and Manic Miner as a subterranean arcade puzzler, but distinguished by its sheer speed. Even by the standards of its era, the graphics were minimalistic, but utterly compelling gameplay made it a huge hit."

Stuart Wynne

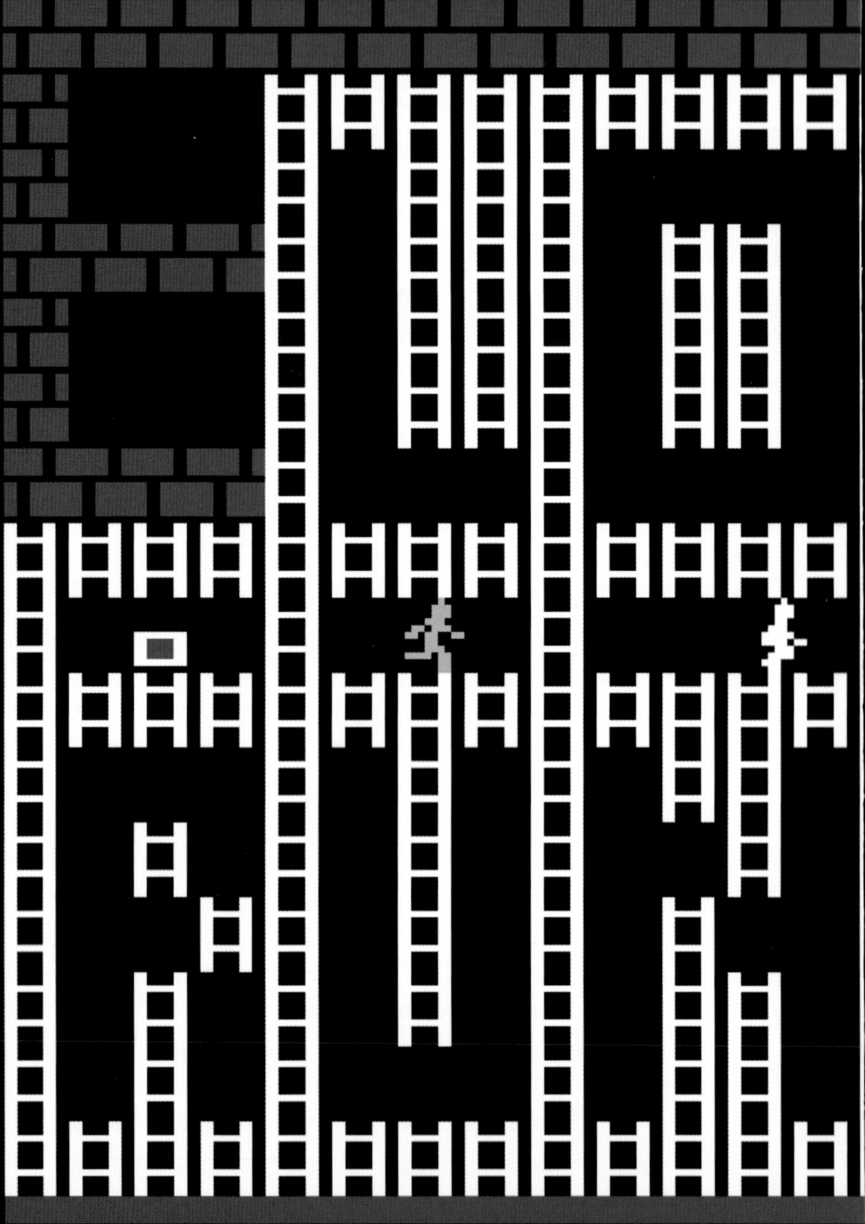

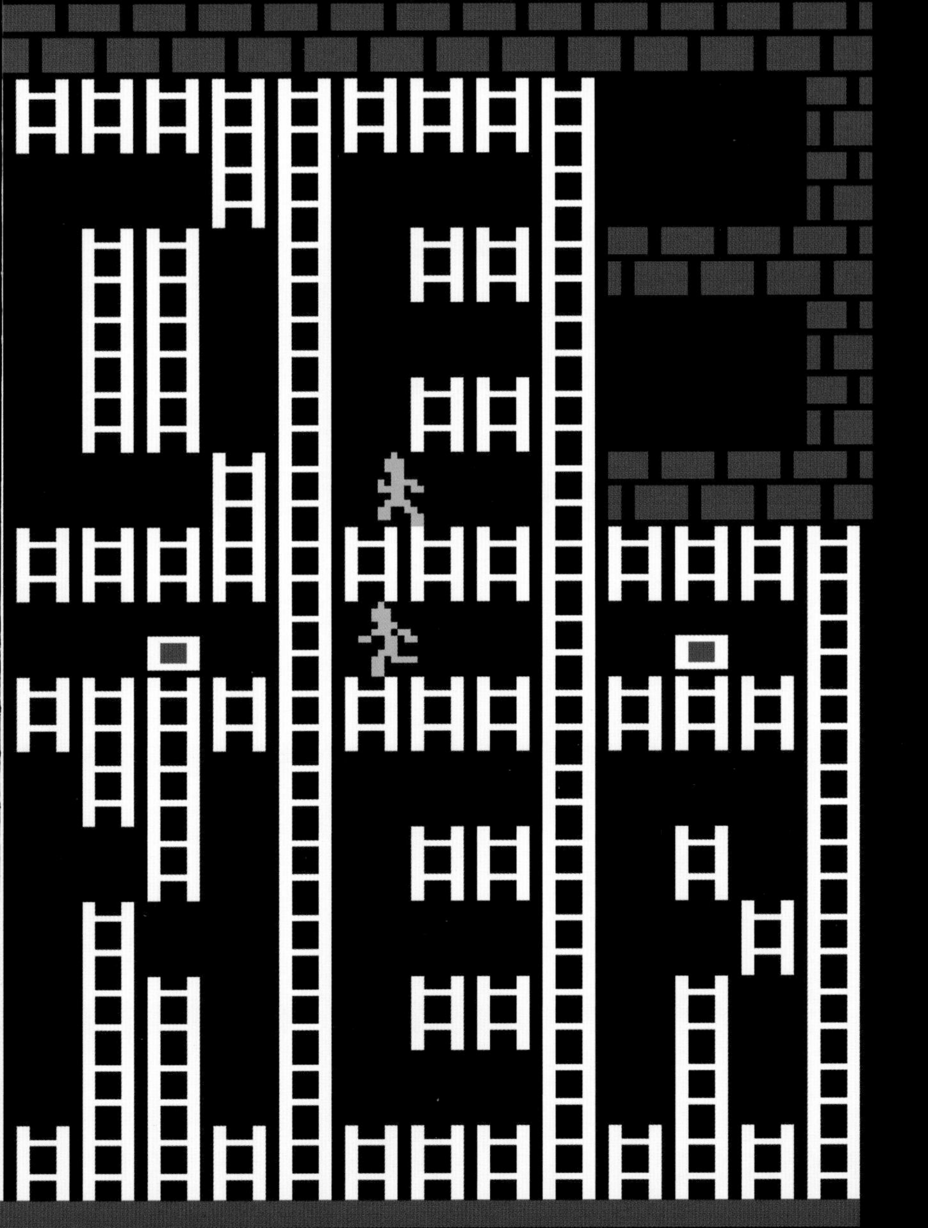

Released
1983

Genre
Platformer

Developer
Douglas E. Smith

Publisher
Brøderbund

M.U.L.E.

"In 1983, game designer Dan Bunten of Ozark Softscape created a game which established computer gaming as a social event way ahead of its time. Turn-based strategy is mixed smartly with action elements, embedded in an intricate economics simulation. Up to four players compete and collude in the colonisation of the distant planet Irata. A plethora of well-balanced random events badger the colonists during their 12-month journey and make each tournament unique. This constitutes the everlasting magic of M.U.L.E."

Christian A. Schiller

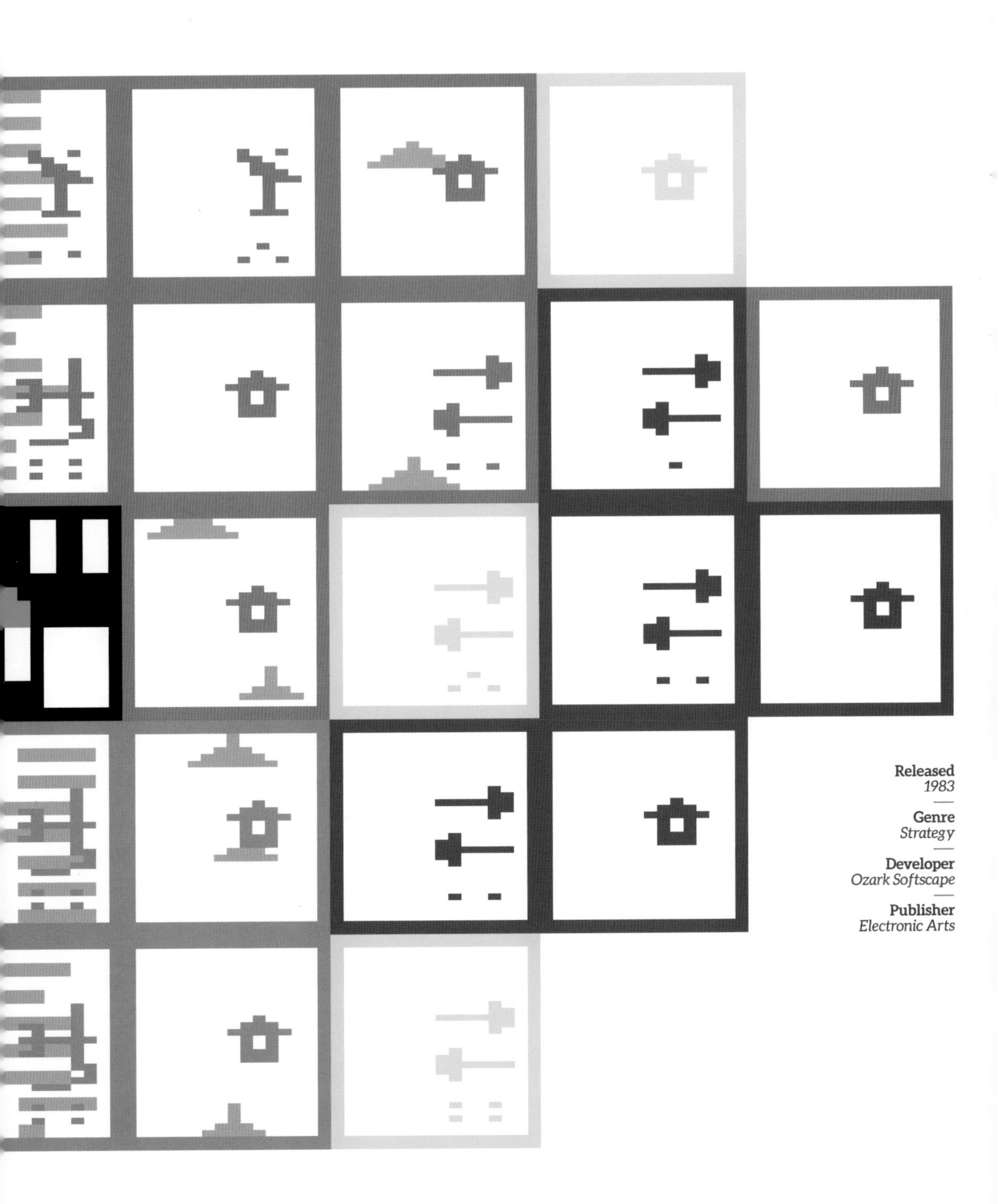

Released
1983

Genre
Strategy

Developer
Ozark Softscape

Publisher
Electronic Arts

Spy Hunter

"Dun-dun da-dun dada-dun dah-dun. Don't deny humming that immediately when seeing the screenshot, you liar. Bally Midway's vertical scrolling car-based shooter may not have set the world on fire graphically, but every vehicle has a personality and vibe surrounding it, especially the poor cyclists when you nudge them! With smooth scrolling and hard but balanced gameplay, the C64 conversion was arguably more playable than its arcade parent."

Mat Allen

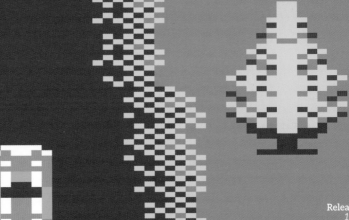

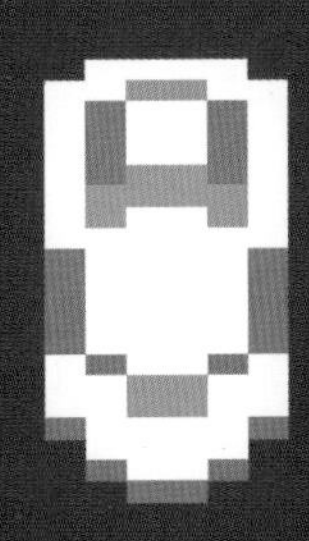

Released
1983

Genre
Arcade

Developer
Sega

Publisher
U.S. Gold

Released
1984

Genre
Action puzzle

Developers
Peter Liepa
Chris Gray

Publisher
First Star Software, Inc.

Boulder Dash®

"These days 'creative technology' is almost commonplace, but back in the day it seemed relatively rare. Boulder Dash was one of the first times in my life where I was able to draw on both my artistic-creative and technical-mathematical sides. It was as if separate poles had merged into a single whole. I wrote the original version for the Atari 400/800 and it was then ported to other platforms by various developers. The C64 conversion was by far the most faithful to the original."

Peter Liepa

Released
1984

Genre
Scrolling shooter

Developer
Archer MacLean

Publisher
U.S. Gold

Dropzone

"After getting my degree with the minimum amount of work, I decided to try and produce a game which at least equalled the quality, speed and gameplay of the arcade games of the time. So I took inspiration from Scramble, Defender, Stargate, Galaxian and many others and went for it. It took me about six months to come up with something looking so good it could be an arcade cabinet."

Archer MacLean

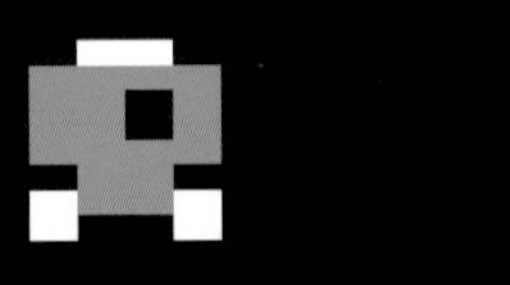

Bruce Lee

"Bruce Lee remains a firm favourite with C64 enthusiasts 30 years after its original release. A unique blend of beat 'em up and platform game, it took players on an epic flick-screen adventure into the heart of a mysterious Wizard's fortress to find the secret of immortality. In a novel twist, the game allowed a second player to assume the role of the bad guys and attempt to thwart Bruce's progress; the result was fiendishly fun and extremely addictive."

Andy Roberts

Released
1984

Genre
Platformer

Developer
Datasoft Inc.

Publisher
U.S. Gold

GH STE

Ghostbusters

"Many people remember the title screen of Ghostbusters more than the game itself. Artist Hilary Mills drew a perfect Ghostbusters logo and the late Russell Lieblich made an instrumental arrangement of the Ghostbusters theme song. Unable to leave it at that I engineered speech for the C64 in order to enable the game to yell 'Ghostbusters!' Add the song lyrics and a follow-the-bouncing-ball animation, and the title screen became one of the most memorable parts of the game."

David Crane

I AIN'T 'FRAI

IF YOU'RE SE

USTERS

O OF NO GHOST!

ING THINGS

Released
1984

Genre
Strategy

Developer
David Crane

Publisher
Activision

Released
1984

Genre
Racing

Developer
Epyx

Publisher
U.S. Gold

Pitstop II

"Pitstop II was something of a technical tour de force back in 1984, with its fast, pseudo-3D courses, convincing car movement and head-to-head split-screen play (although this was offset slightly by the slowest, fiddliest pit stops of all time). The strobing courses and drone of the cars made for a real zen-like racing experience, and I remember having some tense races against the computer opponent. With a Grand Prix mode and multiple tracks, Pitstop II really set the mould for modern racing games."

Steve Jarratt

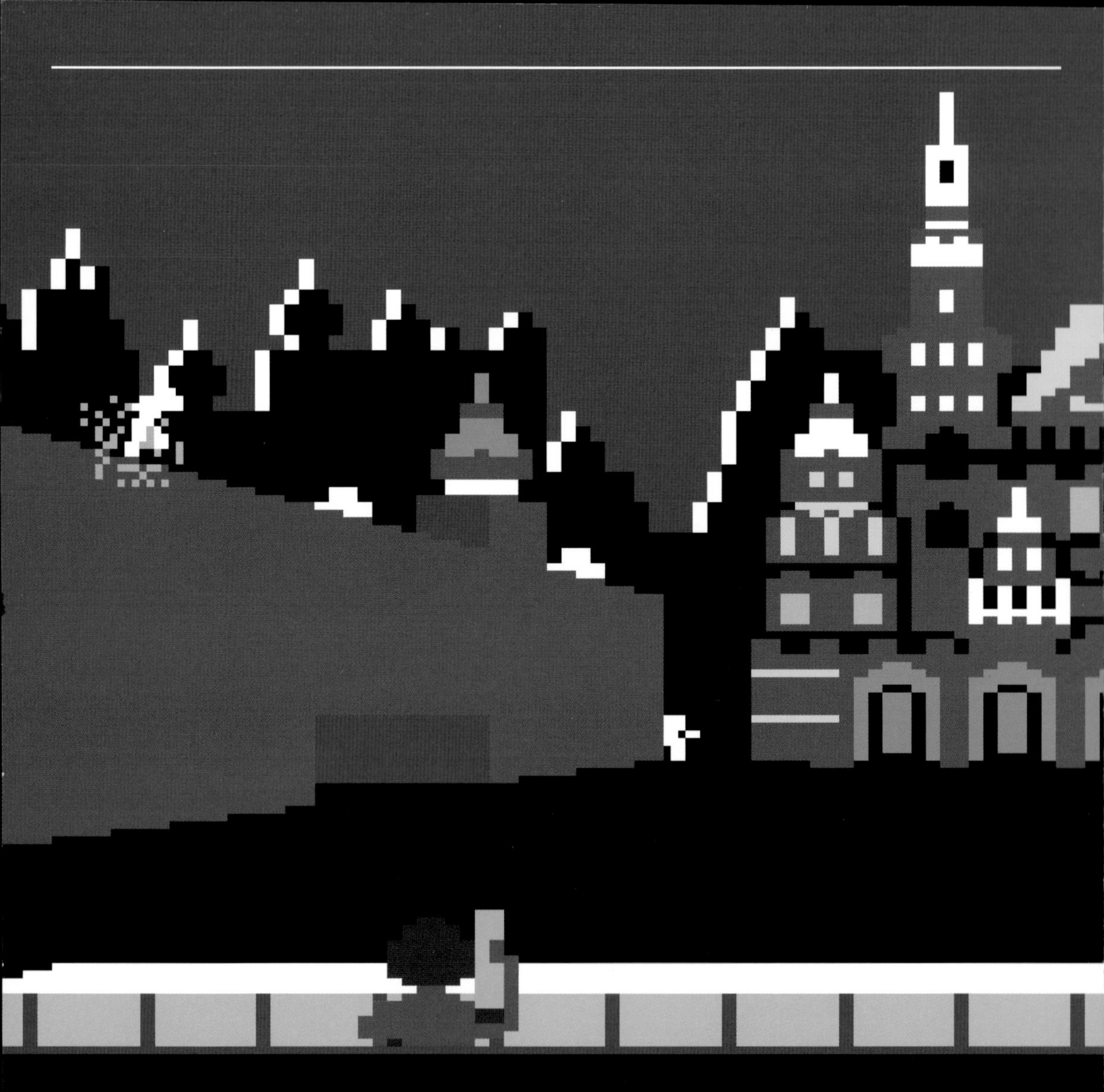

Raid Over Moscow

"Raid Over Moscow immersed the player in the 1980's Cold War conflict between the USA and Russia. As a nuclear missile hurtled toward US soil, the player was tasked with destroying multiple Russian missile silos, infiltrating the Kremlin, and neutralising the nuclear threat. From the Zaxxon-inspired attack run to the 3D bazooka section, the game was years ahead of its time, boasting incredible animation and stunning attention to detail that would become classic hallmarks of

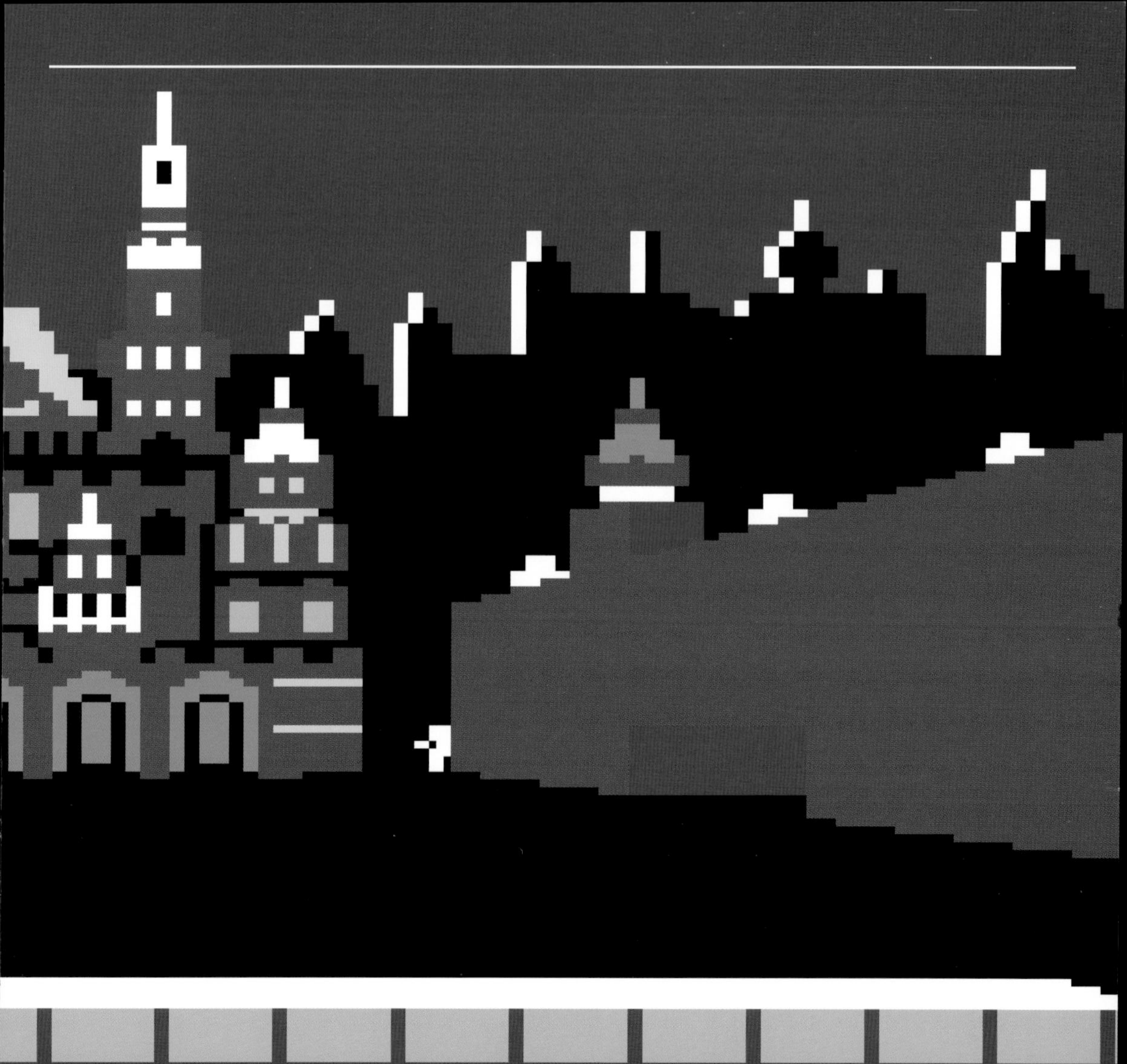

Released
1984

Genre
Shooter

Developer
Access Software

Publisher
U.S. Gold

Impossible Mission

"Another classic from Epyx, which intoned the gamer to 'Stay a while... Stay forever!' with its amazing digitised speech. Impossible Mission was a beautiful exercise in platform gaming, requiring dexterity and timing to guide your somersaulting agent past Elvin Atombender's guardian robots. The level of precision required to complete the game, plus the pressure of a countdown timer made it a tense affair – and I still recall the sheer relief as I finally managed to complete the password puzzle and confront the evil genius with just seconds to spare."

Steve Jarratt

Released
1984

Genre
Platformer

Developer
Epyx

Publisher
U.S. Gold

Park Patrol

"Activision released a solid body of slick, original and playable work in the '80s, including this gem by Tony Ngo featuring jolly tunes from Russell Lieblich. Your duty as a ranger (a choice of boy or girl) is to patrol the park and pick up litter, avoiding turtles, logs and snakes, and saving drowning swimmers. It's a cute, frenetic, fun medley of running and jumping on land and zipping around the river in a rubber dinghy (which is, curiously, reminiscent of Defender)."

Gary Penn

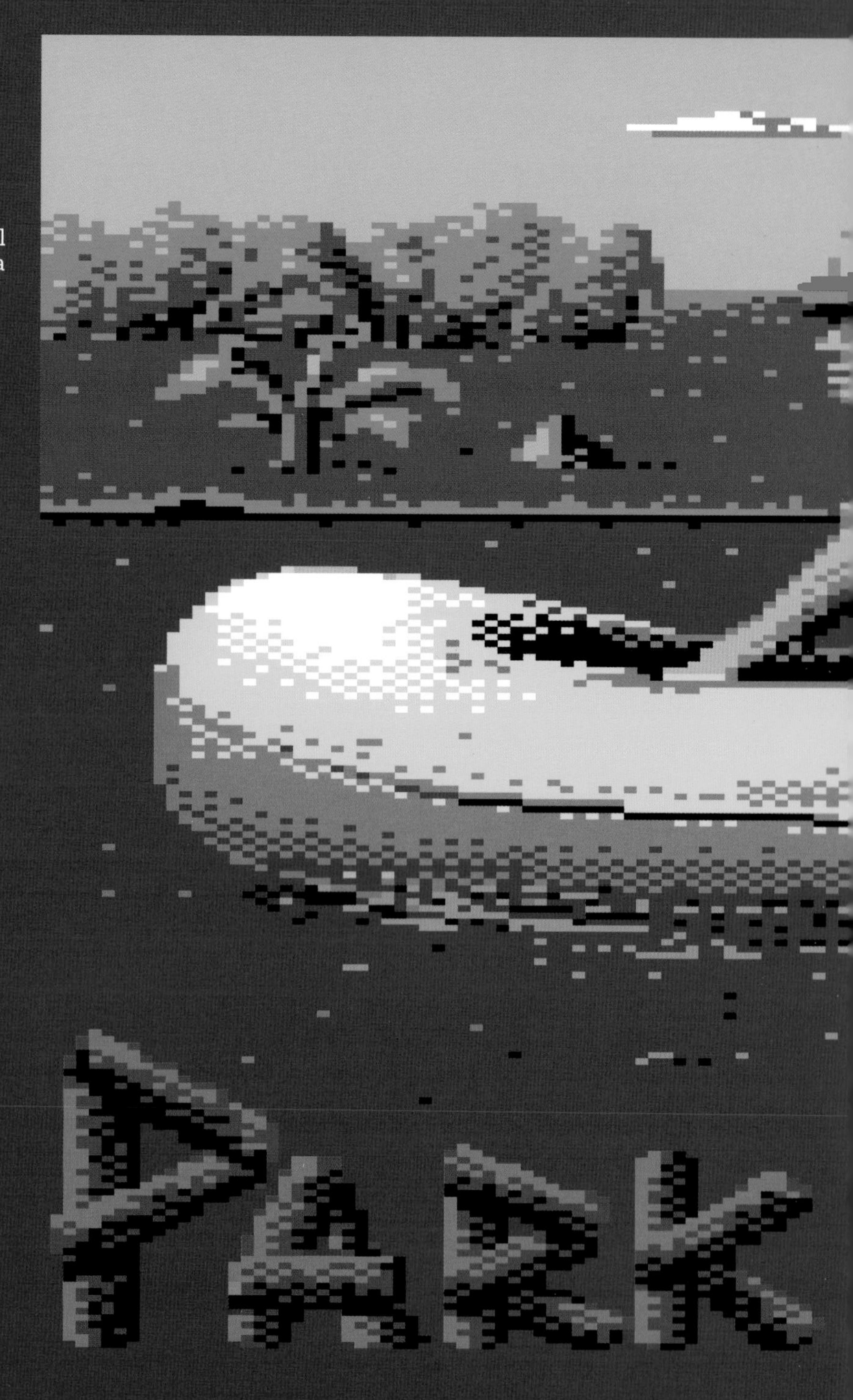

Released
1984

Genre
Action

Developer
Tony Ngo

Publisher
Activision

PATROL

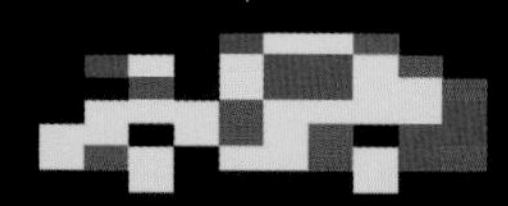

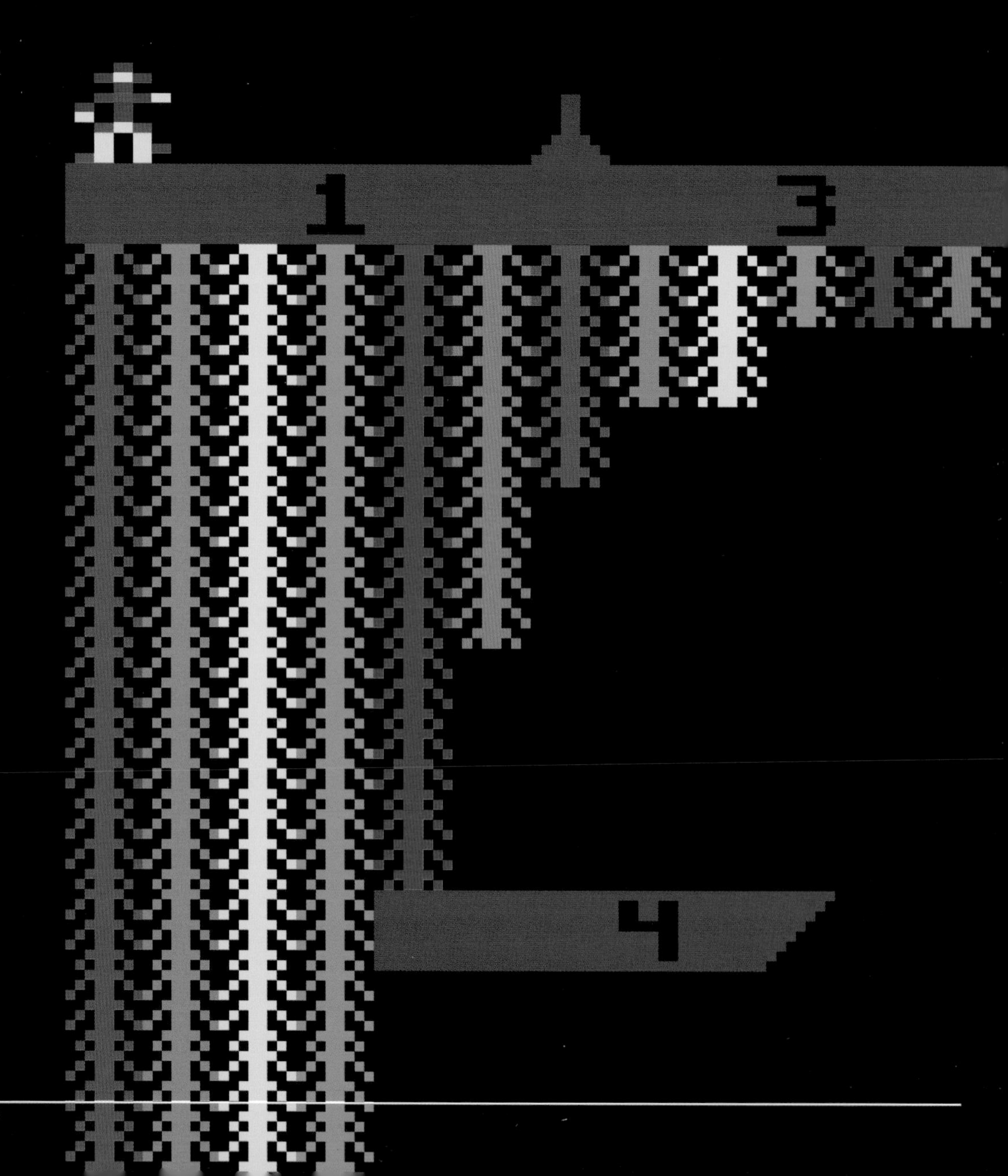
1
3
4

Space Taxi

"I wrote Space Taxi in my freshman year at Hopkins. Once I had the initial framework I was building one to two levels per day. When released, it received several awards, industry recognitions and was particularly praised for its digitised speech. The speech saying 'Hey Taxi!' and all the other phrases are actually my own voice captured on homemade electronics and played back at different speeds to create higher and lower pitch voices."

John F. Kutcher

Released
1984

Genre
Arcade

Developer
John F. Kutcher

Publisher
Muse Software

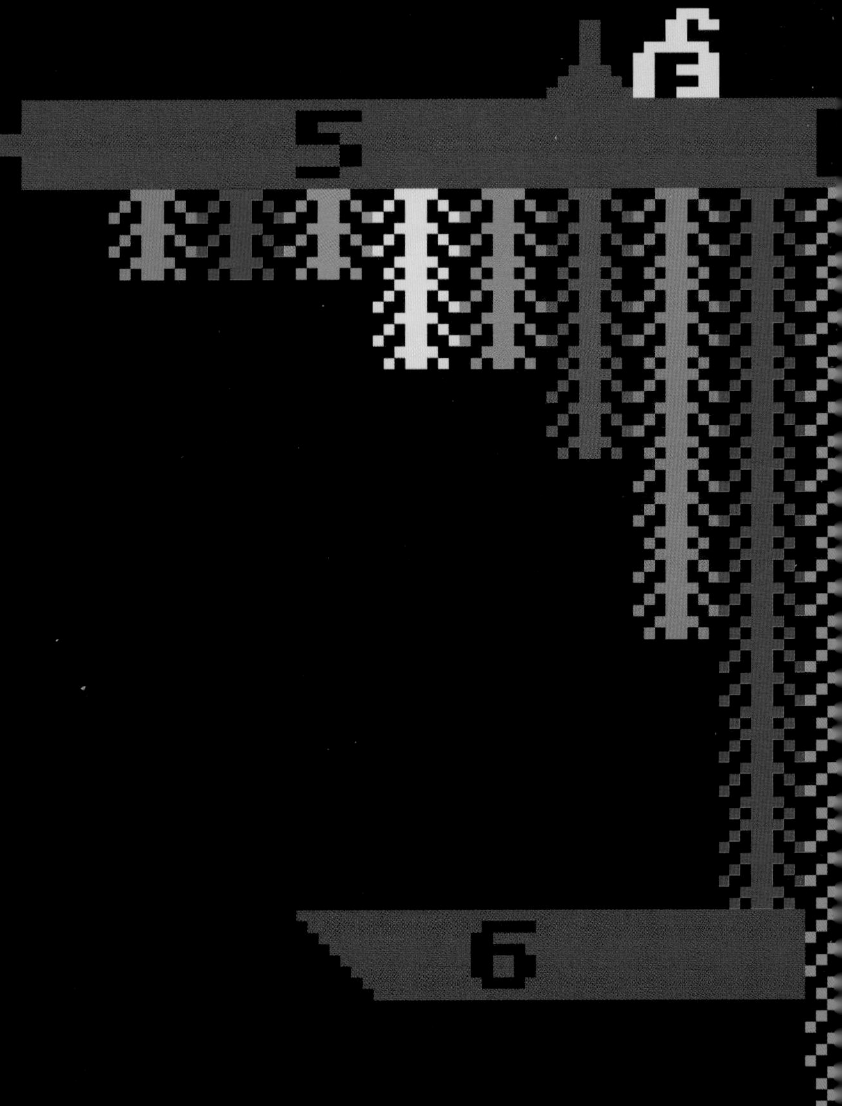

WHITE
BLACK

Spy vs Spy

"Simple, yet characterful line drawings and a text-free, kill-or-be-killed high concept made Mad Magazine's 1961 Spy vs Spy strip perfect for 8-bit gaming. First Star Software's split-screen, two-player design and a host of suitably lethal, comedic traps enjoyed smash-hit success and two sequels. 29 years later it was revived on iOS with lavishly updated, full colour graphics that somehow didn't quite match the charm of the 1984 original."

Stuart Wynne

Released
1984

Genre
Strategy

Developer
Michael Riedel

Publisher
First Star Software, Inc.

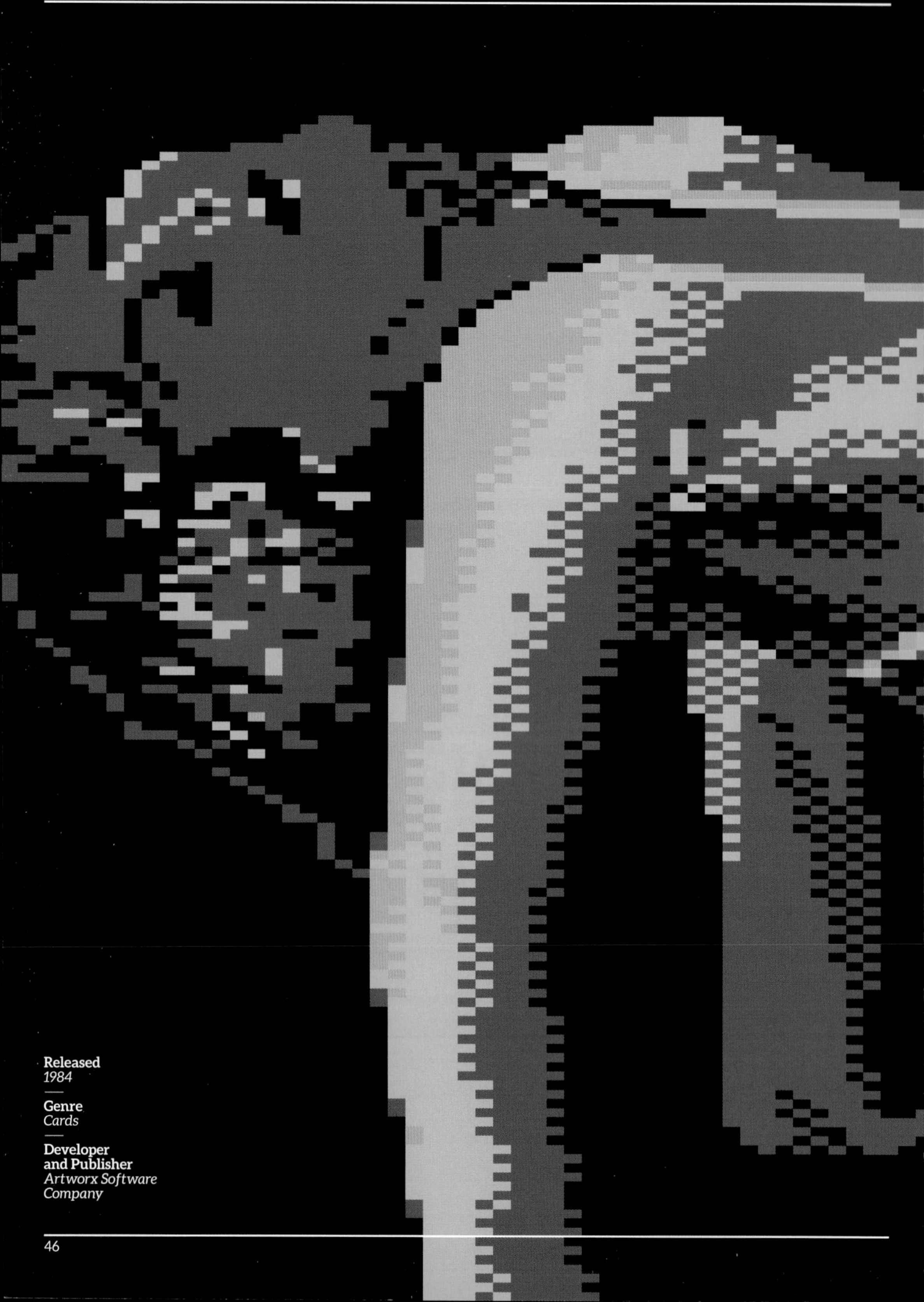

Released
1984

Genre
Cards

Developer and Publisher
Artworx Software Company

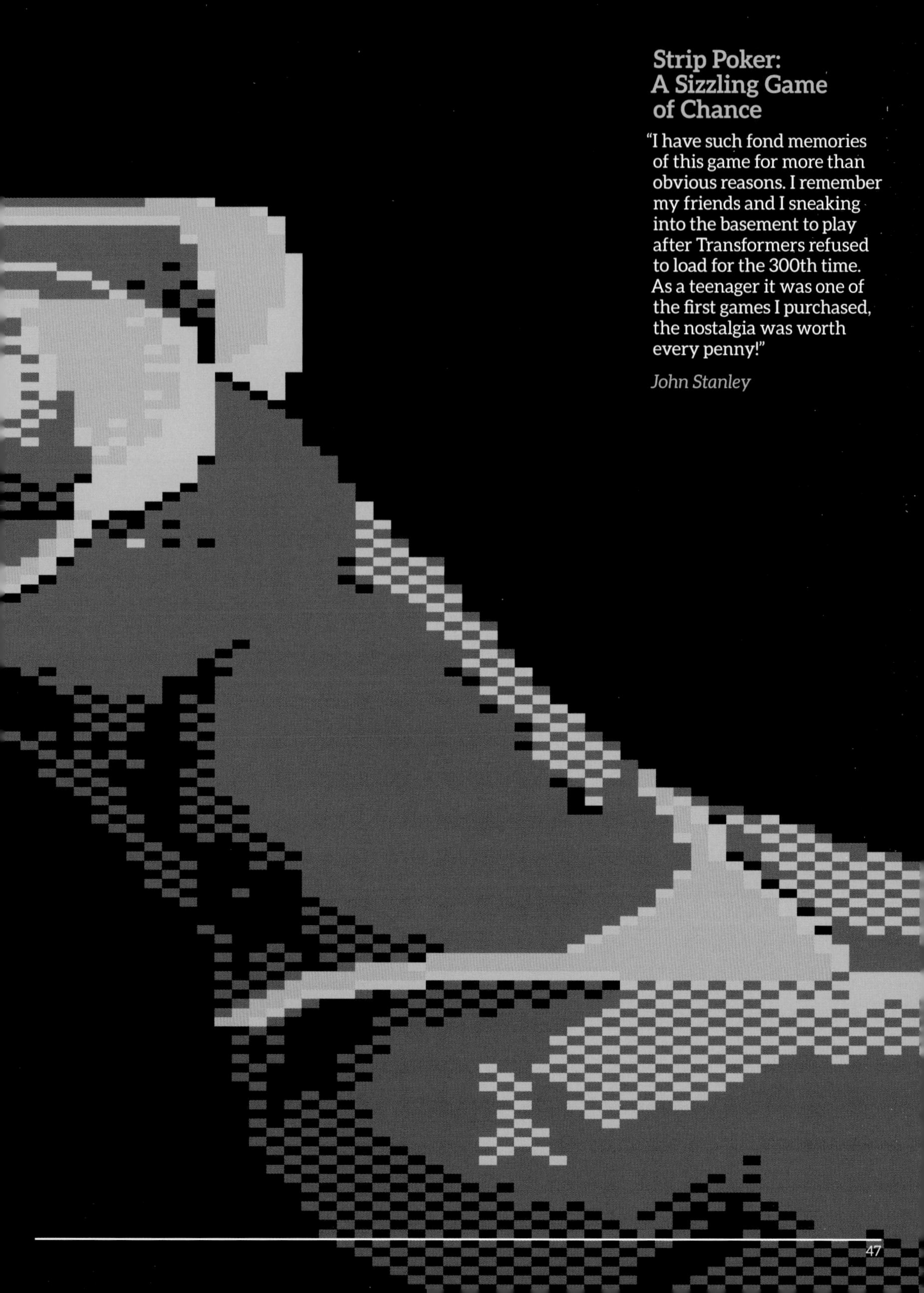

Strip Poker: A Sizzling Game of Chance

"I have such fond memories of this game for more than obvious reasons. I remember my friends and I sneaking into the basement to play after Transformers refused to load for the 300th time. As a teenager it was one of the first games I purchased, the nostalgia was worth every penny!"

John Stanley

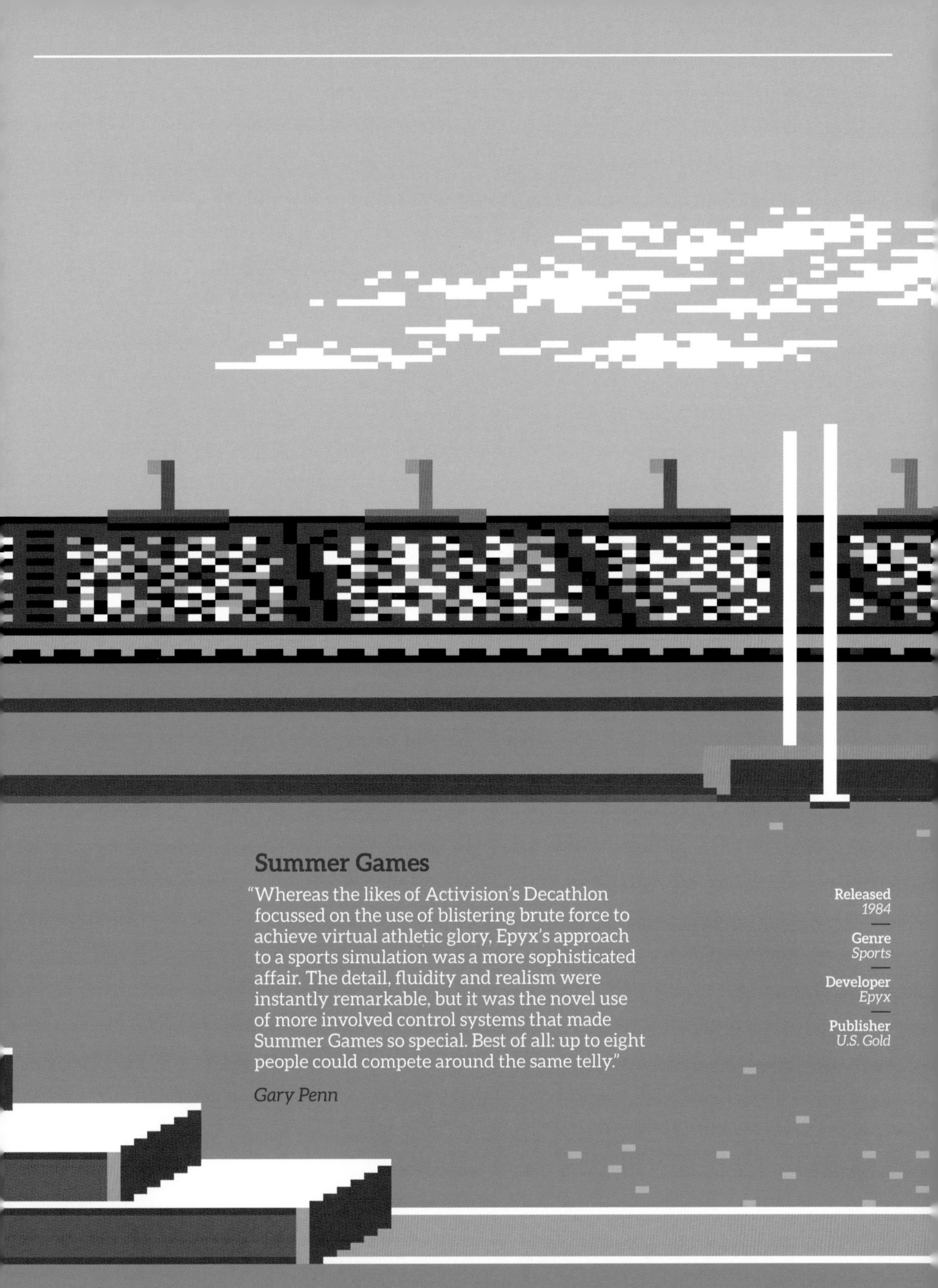

Summer Games

"Whereas the likes of Activision's Decathlon focussed on the use of blistering brute force to achieve virtual athletic glory, Epyx's approach to a sports simulation was a more sophisticated affair. The detail, fluidity and realism were instantly remarkable, but it was the novel use of more involved control systems that made Summer Games so special. Best of all: up to eight people could compete around the same telly."

Gary Penn

Released
1984

Genre
Sports

Developer
Epyx

Publisher
U.S. Gold

1

Bounty Bob Strikes Back!

"Both Bill Hogue's Miner 2049er and this sequel are coarse to the eyes, ears and fingers (and nails-hard to boot). And yet... There's something about these games that just doesn't let go. The 25 stages see you painting platforms in your wake to win, punctuated by jumping, teleporting, sliding down slopes, climbing ladders and collecting objects to make roaming 'monsters' temporarily killable. The high score table assembled by little birds is a delight to behold."

Gary Penn

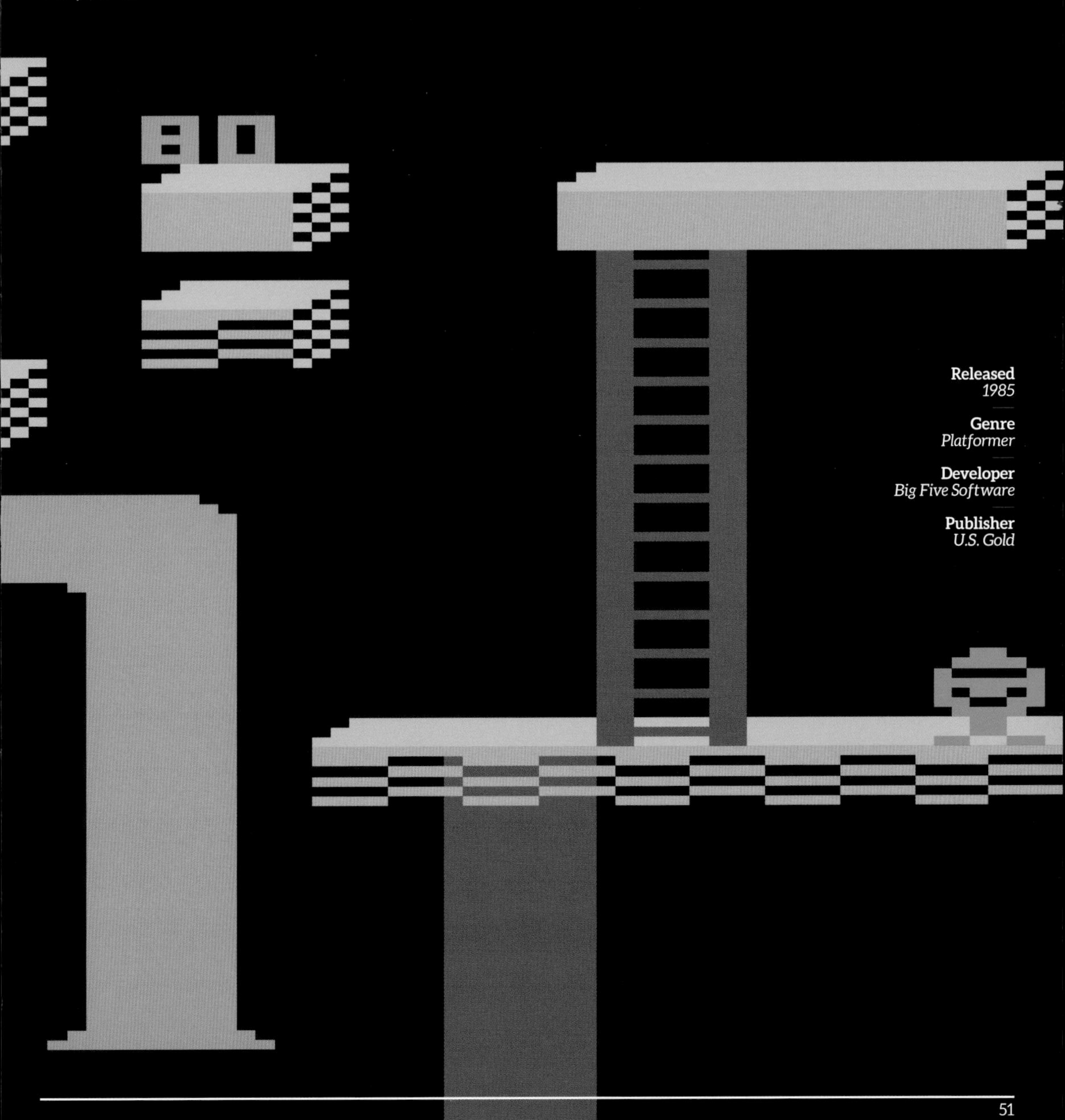

Released
1985

Genre
Platformer

Developer
Big Five Software

Publisher
U.S. Gold

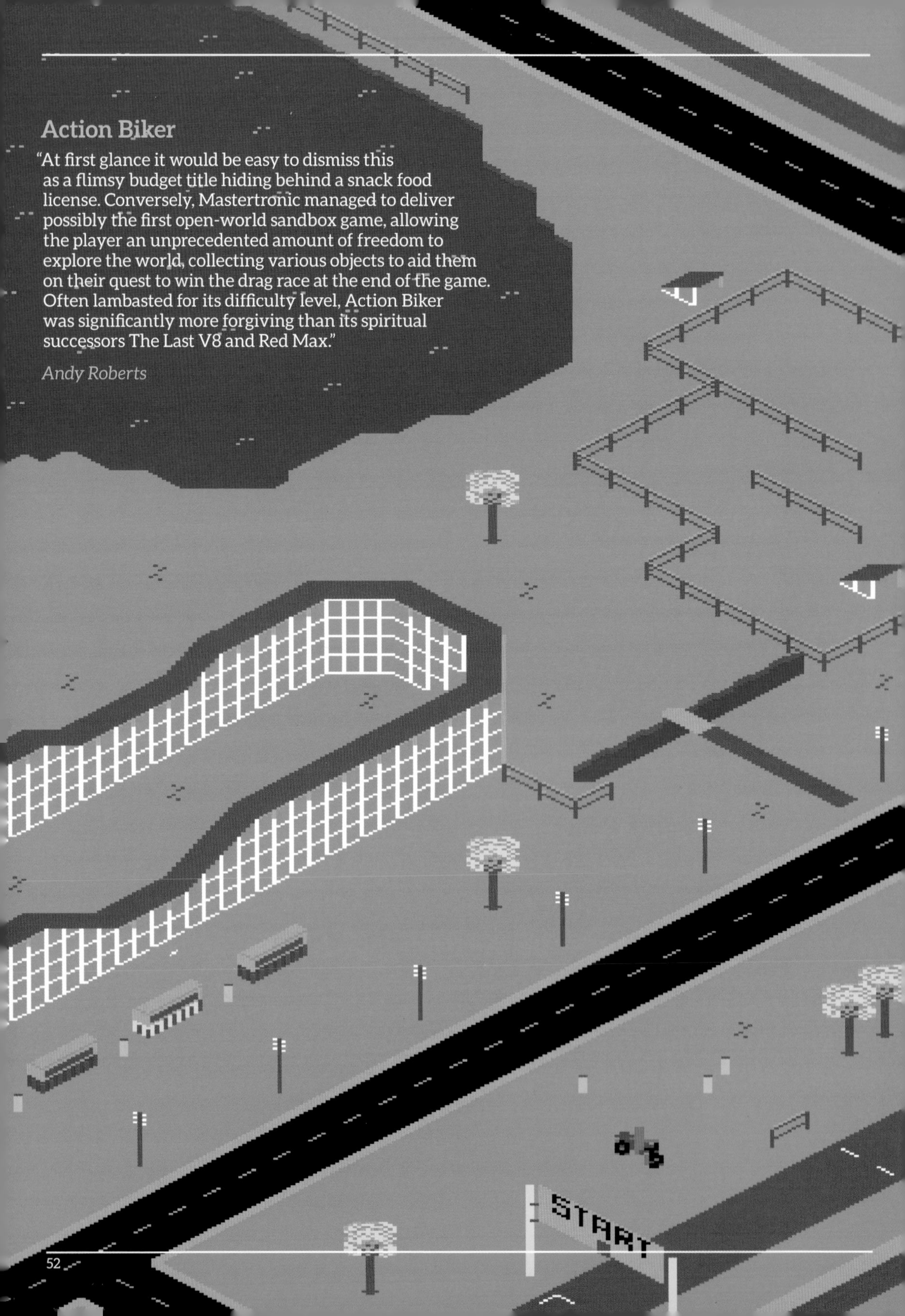

Action Biker

"At first glance it would be easy to dismiss this as a flimsy budget title hiding behind a snack food license. Conversely, Mastertronic managed to deliver possibly the first open-world sandbox game, allowing the player an unprecedented amount of freedom to explore the world, collecting various objects to aid them on their quest to win the drag race at the end of the game. Often lambasted for its difficulty level, Action Biker was significantly more forgiving than its spiritual successors The Last V8 and Red Max."

Andy Roberts

Released
1985

Genre
Action

Developer and Publisher
Mastertronic

Beyond the Forbidden Forest

Released
1985

Genre
Action

Developer
COSMI

Publisher
U.S. Gold

Artwork
Oliver Frey

Beach-Head II: The Dictator Strikes Back

Released
1985

Genre
Shooter

Developer
Access Software

Publisher
U.S. Gold

Artwork
Oliver Frey

FS
AS
FU
CT
LT
AL
EL

Elite

"Though Zzap!64 hadn't even launched, Firebird took the magazine's imminent arrival seriously enough to send Colin Fuidge all the way to our offices in Yeovil. There was never any doubt from the first moments of playing the game – Bob Wade was only dragged away after six hours of non-stop gaming – that Elite would be Zzap!64's first cover, now an iconic image, painted by Oliver Frey. Looking back, the reactions to Elite were spot on, and it has continued to be a game which fascinates generations."

Roger Kean

"Let that word sink in for a moment... Elite. Cover game of issue 1 of Zzap! Gold Medal material right from the off, 30 years ago, 30! The nostalgia and allure of Elite is still immense as is seen with anticipation for Elite: Dangerous. Elite promised infinite space to explore, combat and a sense of wonder and it delivered in style. 3D was never the forte of the C64 and it's awfully lonely out there with minimal sound too, but hey, it's space after all. We were however, enthralled. Elite paved the way for space games like no other. Awesome."

Robin Hogg

Released
1985

Genre
Simulation

Developers
David Braben
Ian Bell

Publisher
Firebird

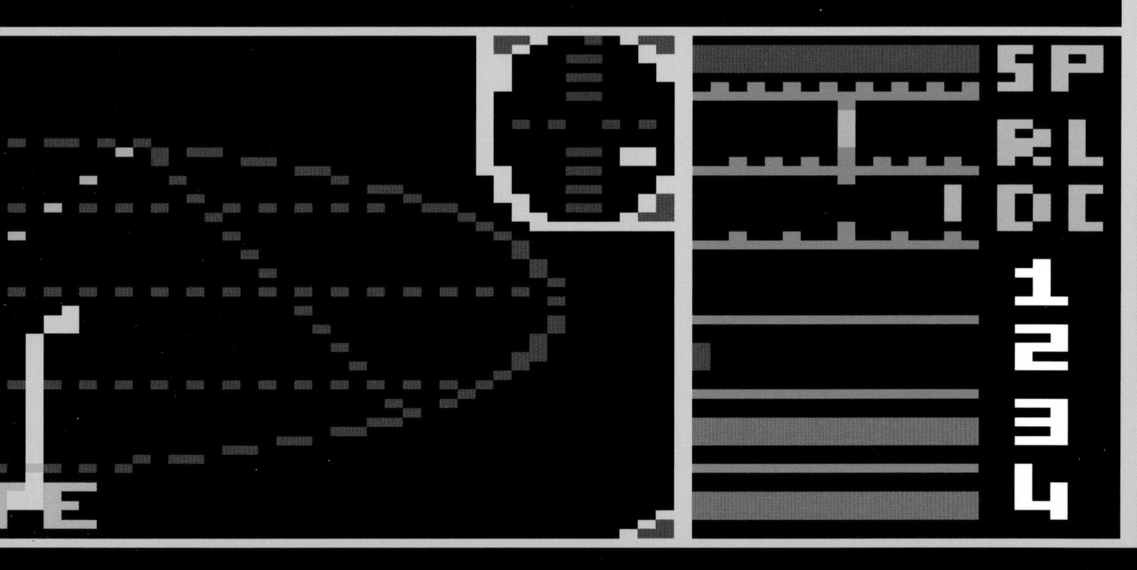

The Eidolon

"The team Gary Winnick, Charlie Kelner and myself played ideas off of each other to create The Eidolon. Gary's characters were the key element of the game and the remainder were mazes, fractals and effects. Ron Gilbert and I joined the games group to provide C64 expertise and we created some impossible effects. Eidolon used full screen sprites and particle models which were revolutionary at the time."

Kevin Furry

Released
1985

Genre
First-person shooter

Developer
Lucasfilm Games

Publisher
Activision

“The palette was really limited and the resolution ultra low but I think people brought their imagination to the games and filled in the detail.”

Hugh Riley, graphic artist

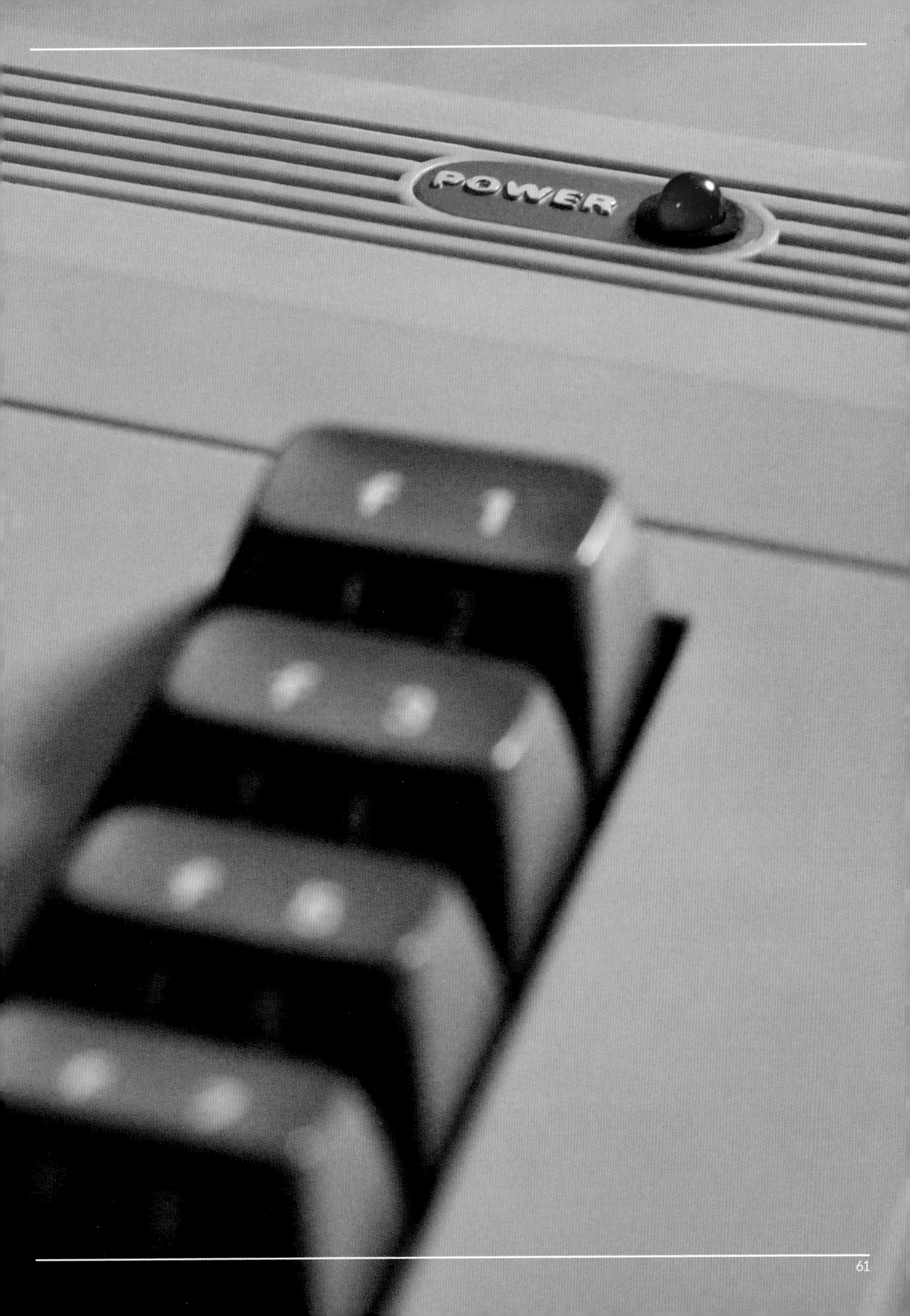
POWER

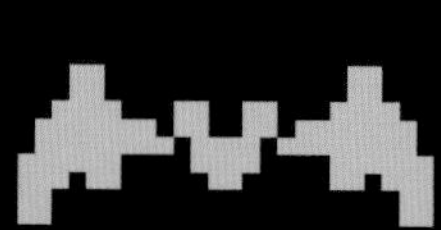

Cauldron

"It would be amusing to think that Palace Software looked at arcade shooter Defender and thought 'Yeah, it's good. But it's not quite 'witchy' enough' and came up with Cauldron. The truth though is that this was instead a clever attempt to fuse two gaming genres – in this case shooting and platforming – and the results were... interesting. All this was tempered by the pain of the excruciatingly high difficulty level which was harsh even by old school standards. More trick than treat."

Andy Dyer

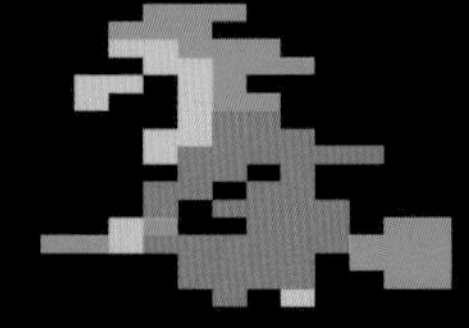

Released
1985

Genre
Action

Developer and Publisher
Palace Software

Hyper Sports

"I recall Hyper Sports even being used for a round of the kids' TV quiz show, First Class. While the C64 game cut out the pole vault and two-player mode, it was a decent coin-op conversion with nice cartoony graphics, all packed into a single load. Each of the six events is a master class in playability: easy to pick up, hard to master. It was a bit of a joystick killer, though!"

Phil King

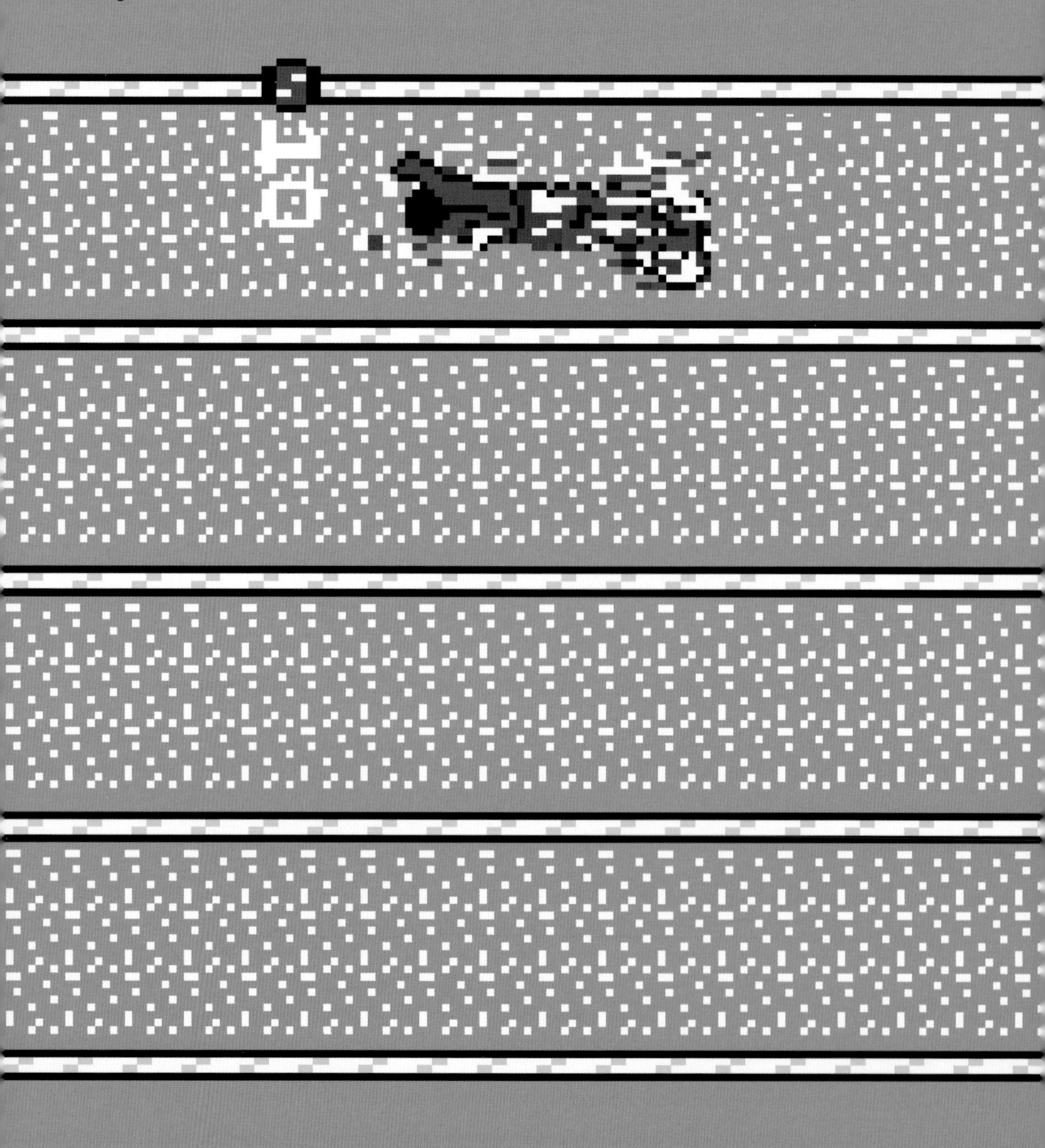

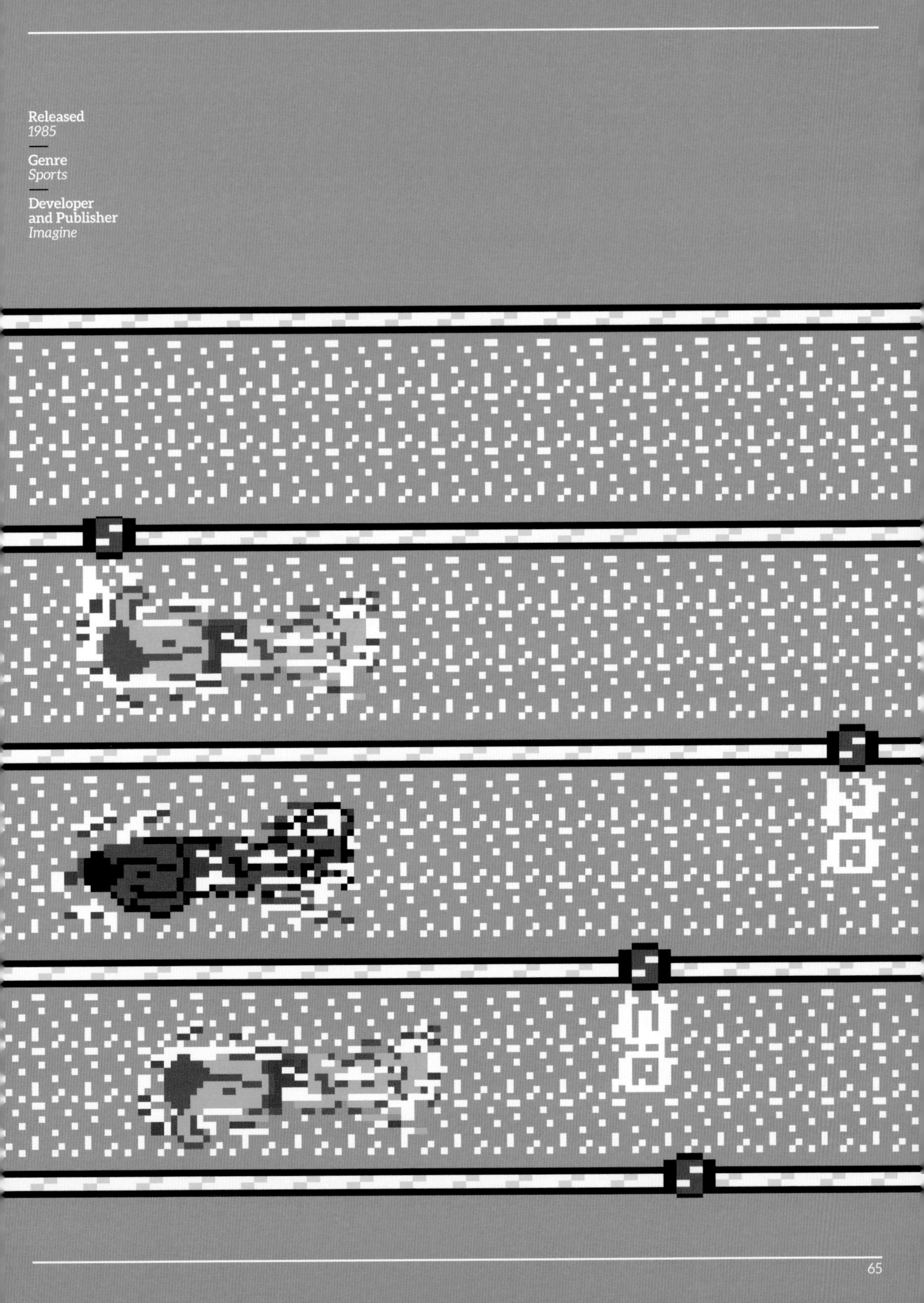

Released
1985

Genre
Sports

Developer and Publisher
Imagine

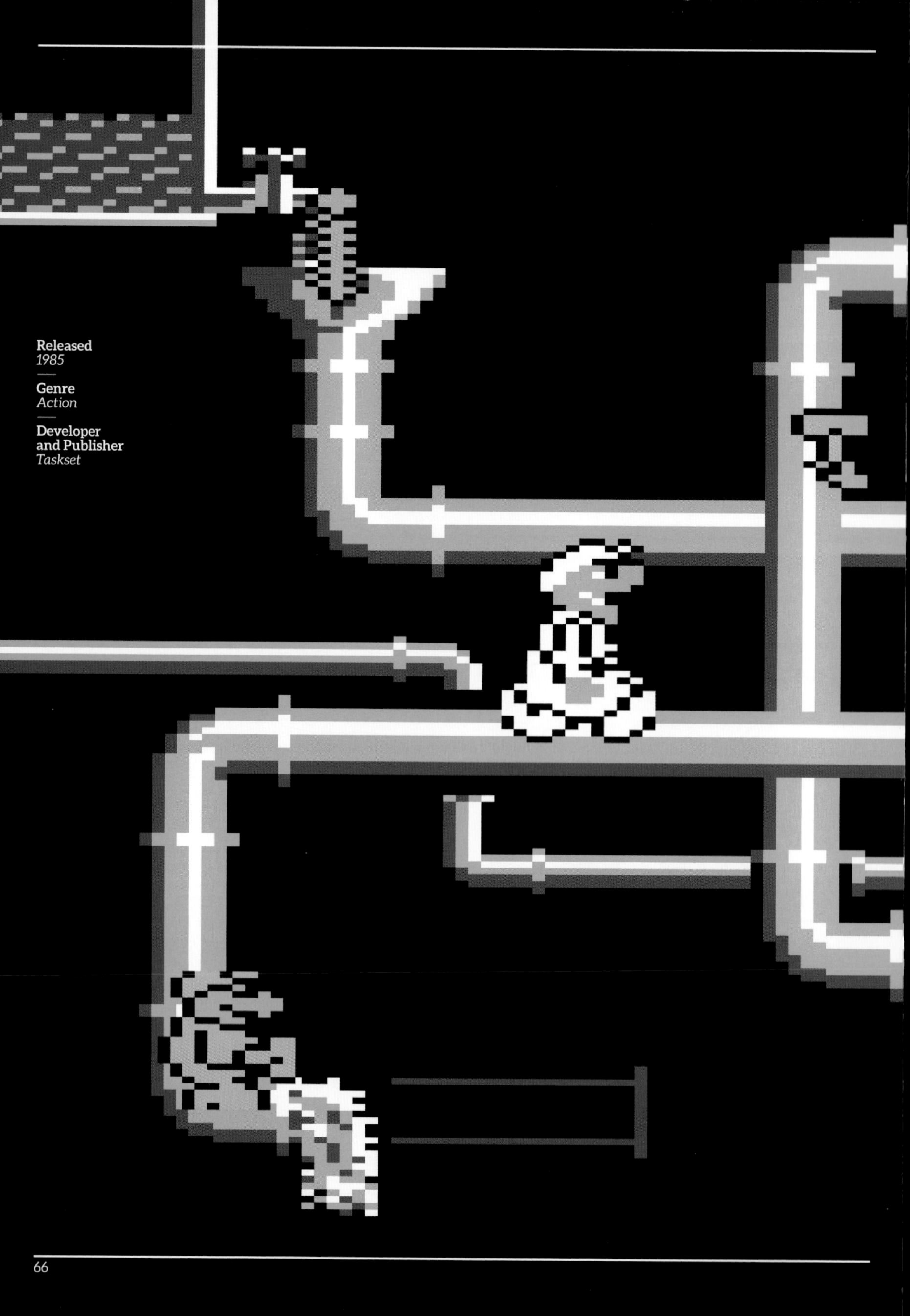

Released
1985

Genre
Action

Developer and Publisher
Taskset

Super Pipeline II

"Sheikh Aleg has a problem, and thus so do you, in keeping his pipelines free from sabotage and interference. The various tools and fauna may look cute, but they'd soon as rip a hole in the pipes and yourself, given a second chance. Nothing that your unlimited supply of Freds can't fix, however, with their trusty Irish screwdrivers. I swear though that lobster ended up moonlighting in Great Giana Sisters later..."

Mat Allen

Kikstart

"Shaun Southern's affectionate, unofficial tribute to the BBC television show Kick Start (the original Mr. Chip release even featured a take on the programme's theme tune) is the spiritual forerunner to the contemporary Trials series. A motorbike is used to negotiate eight different courses, comprising the likes of rough terrain, tyres, cars and buses. Striving for the smoothest possible ride to shave off valuable split seconds from records became an obsession."

Gary Penn

Released
1985

Genre
Racing

Developer
Mr. Chip Software

Publisher
Mastertronic

Monty on the Run

"The third in the Monty Mole series, this is probably one of the best-loved C64 titles, helped in no small part by an epic Rob Hubbard soundtrack. In his quest to outrun the authorities, Monty's adventure would take him through a maze of intricately-crafted screens, collecting essential items and somersaulting from platform to platform. Like many British games from the 1980s, Monty gave subtle nods of respect to the Zeitgeist – and the occasional up yours to the establishment."

Andy Roberts

Released
985

Genre
Platformer

Developer
Micro Projects

Publisher
Gremlin Graphics

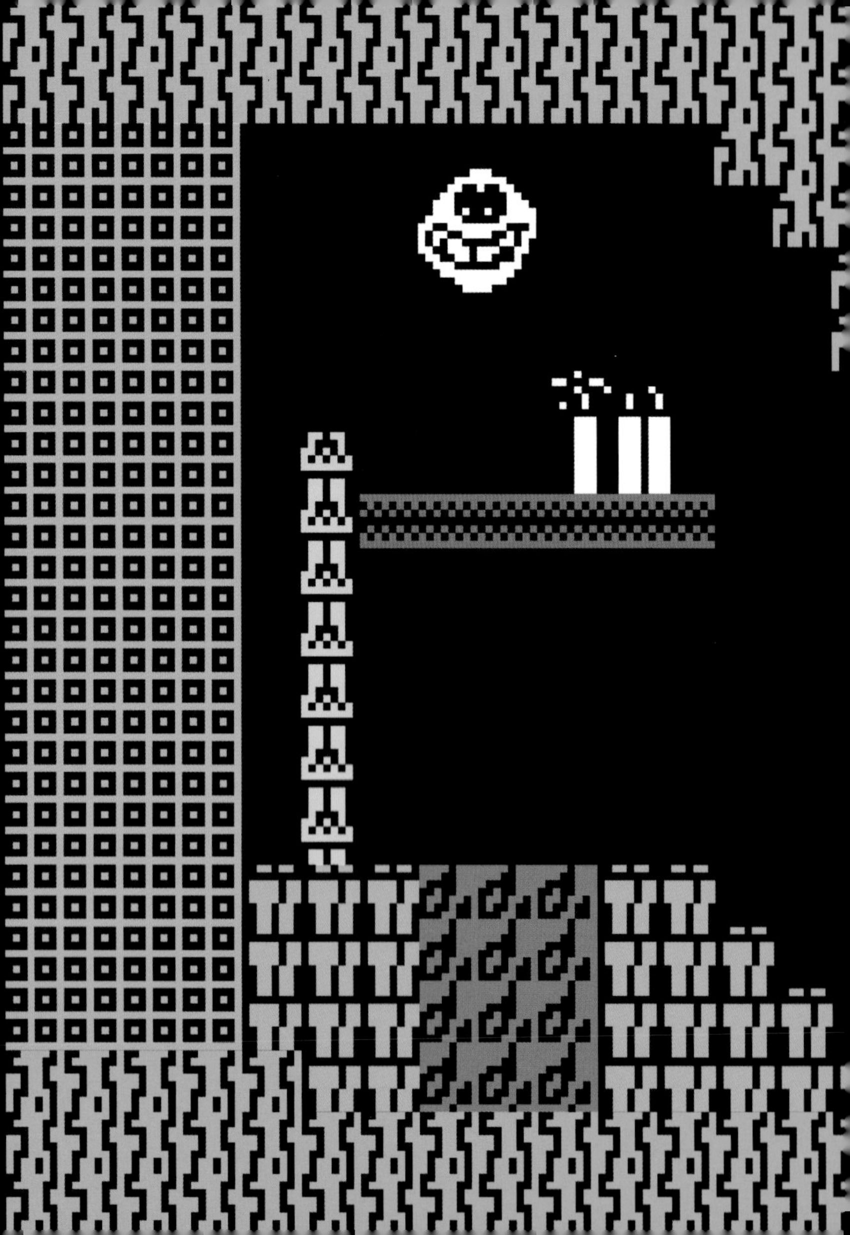

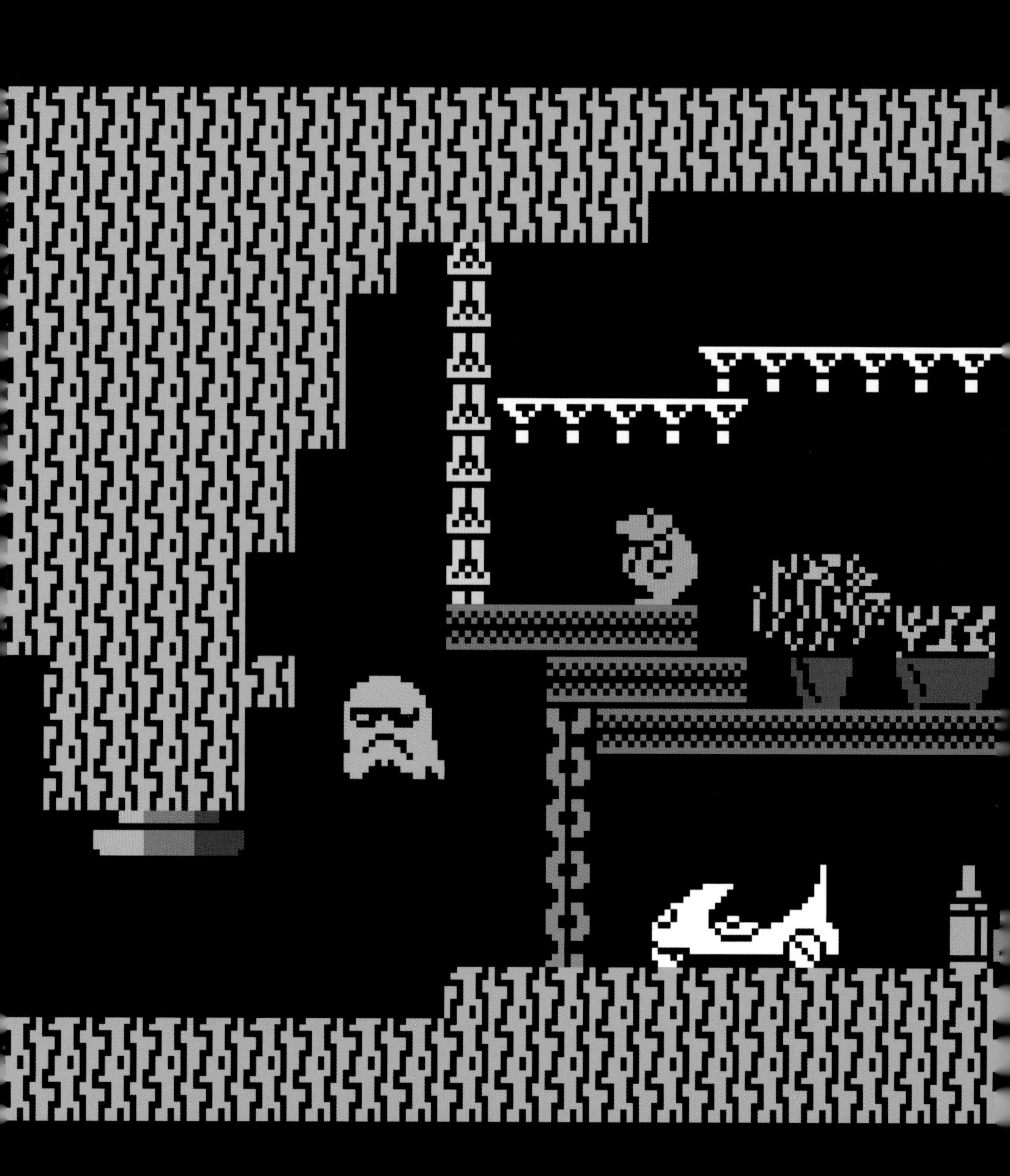

Mercenary

"Before GTA, before Oblivion and Skyrim, there was Paul Woakes' Mercenary. A true open world, sandbox action adventure game, crammed into the C64. The wireframe vector graphics were visually minimalist, but the gameworld was incredibly rich and engaging, with side-quests and a variety of vehicles to pilot and mysteries to solve as you sought to escape from planet Targ. Few C64 games grabbed me like Mercenary did, with its slick 3D graphics, clever twists and wry wit. It gave me a rare glimpse of the future of gaming that wouldn't be fully realised for well over a decade."

Steve Jarratt

Released
1985

Genre
Adventure

Developer and Publisher
Novagen Software

The Way of the Exploding Fist

"Fist's graphics were as realistic as they were elegant, and the digitised sound effects made every round powerfully physical. Its intuitive controls allowed for a natural flow of moves and blocks, so that the computer game karatekas' actions alone determined a fight's outcome: the grin over the first successful roundabout kick is still etched in players' faces. A historic, seismic release in 1985, the depth of gameplay and immersion became the yardstick by which the evolving beat 'em up genre would be judged."

Andreas Wanda

Released
1985

Genre
Fighting

Developer
Beam Software

Publisher
Melbourne House

Released
1985

Genre
Sports

Developer
Epyx

Publisher
U.S. Gold

Frankie goes to Hollywood

"Frankie was a game that felt very different for the time. It was very visual and music based, taking a lot of references from the pop group. I think we were all very happy with the way the game and the graphics turned out. My only regret is the lack of a talking moose in the murder mystery game, something Paul Morley (representative of the band) said no to! Who doesn't want a talking moose head in a game giving out clues!?"

Karen Davies-Downey

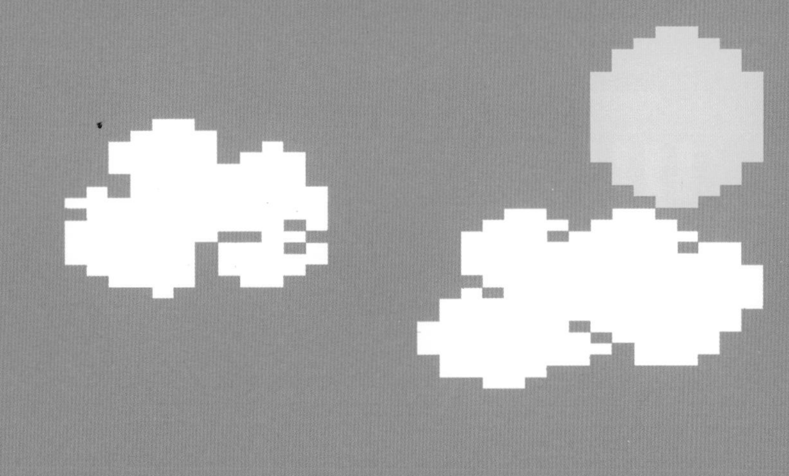

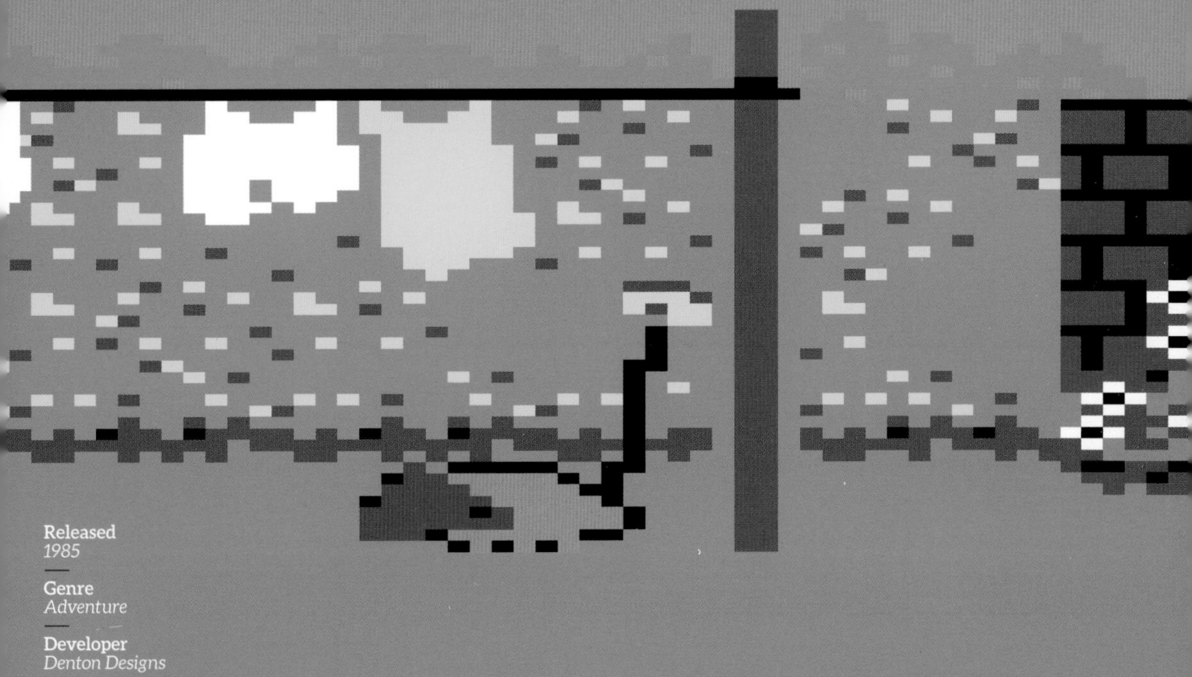

Released
1985

Genre
Adventure

Developer
Denton Designs

Publisher
Ocean

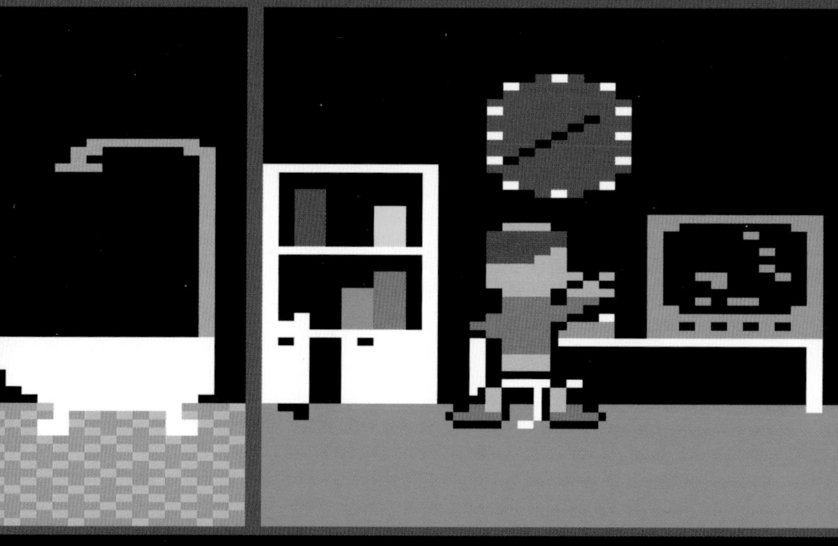

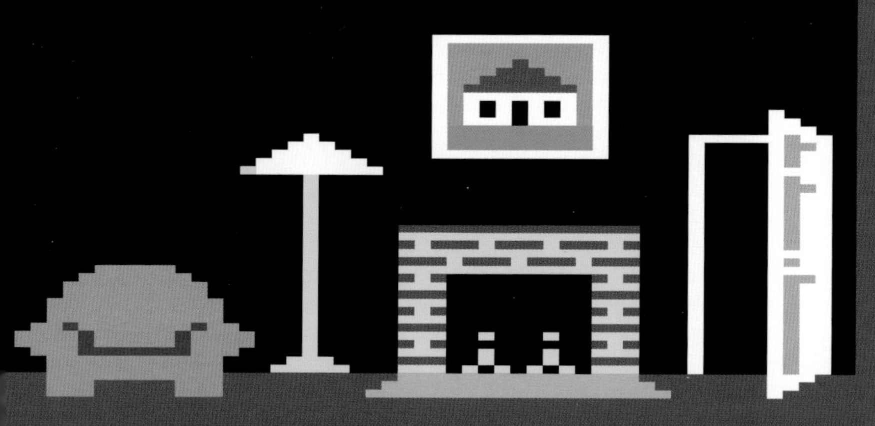

Released
1985

Genre
Simulation

Developer
David Crane

Publisher
Activision

Little Computer People

"Few people realise that the Little Computer People disk already had a custom person on it. This was done by imprinting a unique serial number on each disk to seed their personality. In order for the personality to persist from session to session, a sector of 'brain' data was written to the disk during the game. Beginning in December, if the person played a record there was a chance that he would play Christmas music. The likelihood increased every day until Christmas Day. Since many kids got their copy of Little Computer People as a Christmas gift, many owners never discovered this fact!"

David Crane

Karateka

"I created Karateka while attending Yale in the early 1980s. My goal was to create a game that was visually sophisticated, yet so easy to play that even a non-gamer could immediately pick up the joystick and become addicted. Karateka's success proved to me (and to my parents) that this could be a legitimate career. It helped me decide, right after college, to go on and make Prince of Persia. I was lucky to have Robert Cook to do the Commodore 64 port, he had a great eye for detail in graphics and sound."

Jordan Mechner

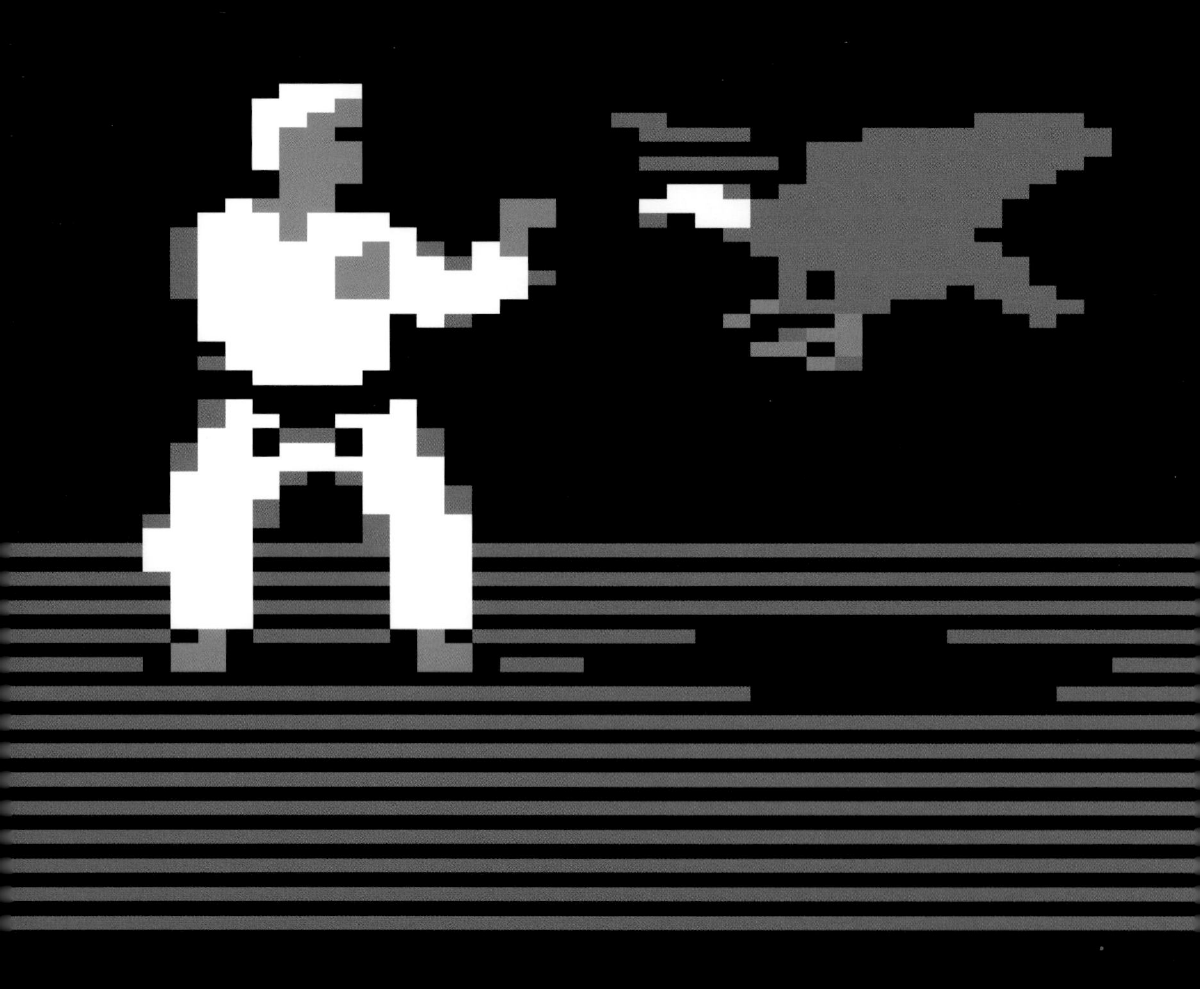

Released
1985

Genre
Scrolling beat 'em up

Developer
Jordan Mechner

Publisher
Brøderbund

Law of the West

"The most interesting game I designed was Law of the West. I incorporated a system in which the player could do bad things – you could shoot lots of people – but it had consequences. And I think that was interesting – to develop a darker story. I also tried to have all the characters react differently to you depending on what you had done previously."

Alan Miller

Released
1985

Genre
Adventure

Developer and Publisher
Accolade

ALERT.
001

Paradroid

"This was our second title for the C64 after Gribbly's Day Out, so it was important for us to deliver a great product. The Paradroid diaries in Zzap!64 had created some good publicity ahead of launch and fortunately Andrew Braybrook delivered a phenomenal game. Paradroid has a beautifully elegant design and is wonderfully balanced. It wasn't actually our biggest ever hit but has certainly become something of a cult classic."

Andrew Hewson

Released
1985

Genre
Puzzle shooter

Developer
Graftgold

Publisher
Hewson Consultants

Thing on a Spring

"Development wasn't going so well on a new C64 game Gremlin were trying to make. We agreed to take on the development and were told we had six weeks to finish it! Around the same time Rob Hubbard had sent us a flyer stating 'Want great music in your games?'. Yes we did! As Rob was unemployed at the time we had to pay for his train travel to meet with us, but he soon delivered on his promise and sent the first draft of the now famous Thing on a Spring title track."

Jason Perkins

Released
1985

Genre
Platformer

Developer
Micro Projects

Publisher
Gremlin Graphics

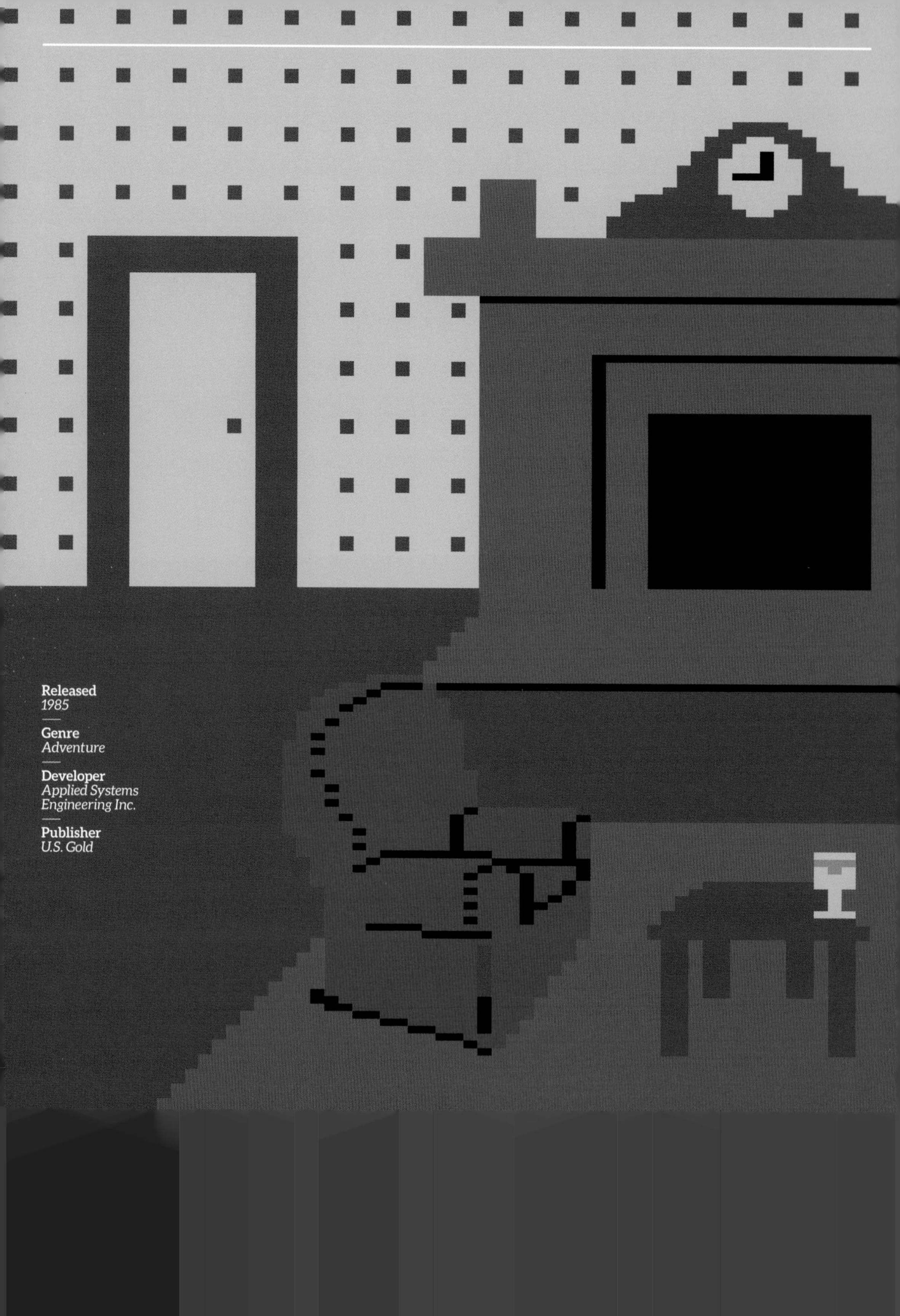

Released
1985

Genre
Adventure

Developer
Applied Systems Engineering Inc.

Publisher
U.S. Gold

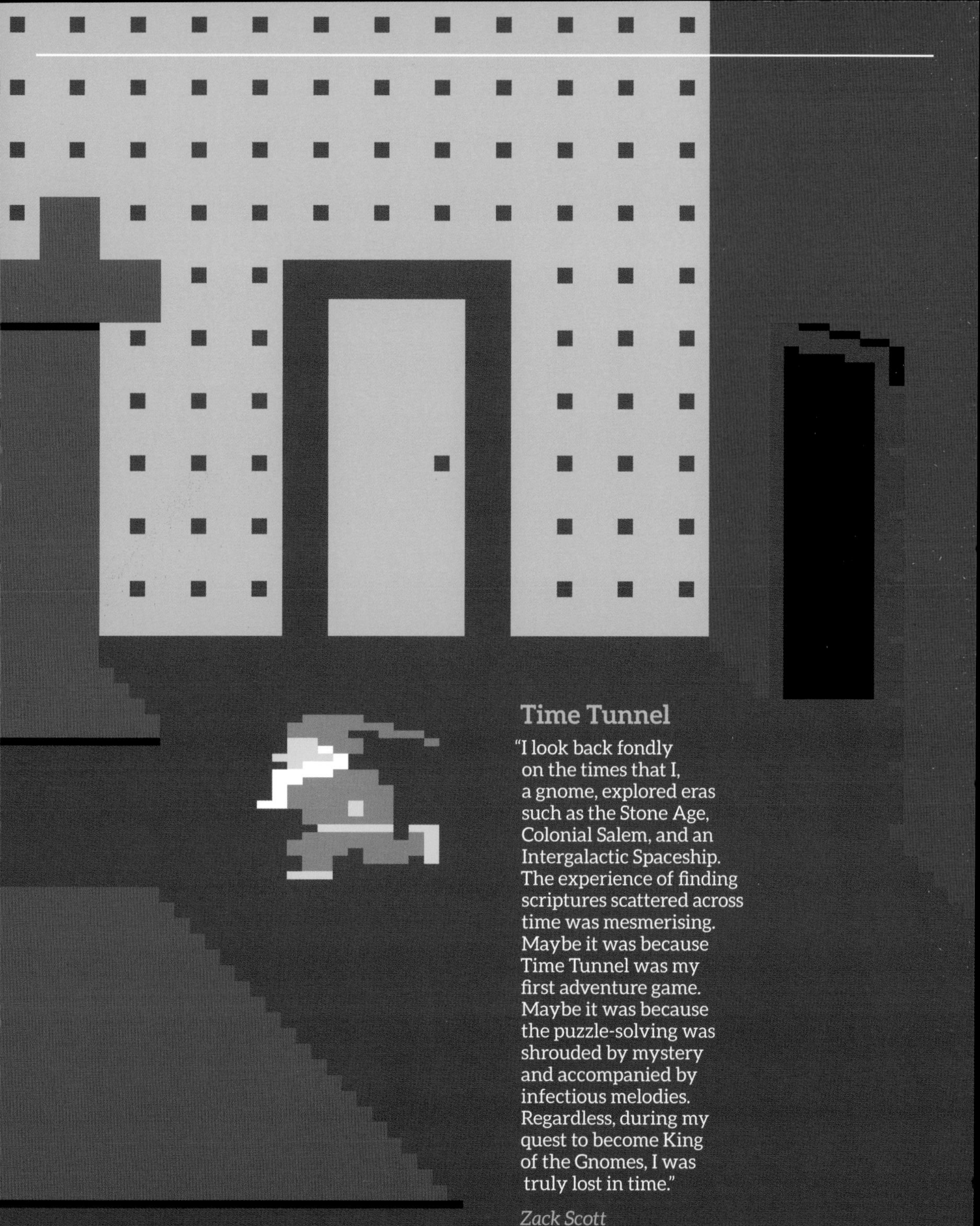

Time Tunnel

"I look back fondly on the times that I, a gnome, explored eras such as the Stone Age, Colonial Salem, and an Intergalactic Spaceship. The experience of finding scriptures scattered across time was mesmerising. Maybe it was because Time Tunnel was my first adventure game. Maybe it was because the puzzle-solving was shrouded by mystery and accompanied by infectious melodies. Regardless, during my quest to become King of the Gnomes, I was truly lost in time."

Zack Scott

Ghosts 'n Goblins

"Capcom's 1985 arcade smash-hit featured exactly the sort of lavish, richly detailed sprites to push the C64 to its limits. In truth, it would take four years and an upgraded (1MB) 16-bit Amiga to fully capture the coin-op, but it was the C64 game with its cut-down levels and ferocious difficulty that was a titan of its era and the perfect game for bragging rights over the rival Sinclair Spectrum."

Stuart Wynne

Released
1986

Genre
Platformer

Developer
Chris Butler

Publisher
Elite Systems

Green Beret

Released
1986

Genre
Run and gun

Developer and Publisher
Imagine

Artwork
Oliver Frey

Leaderboard

Released
1986

Genre
Sports

Developer
Access Software

Publisher
U.S. Gold

Artwork
Oliver Frey

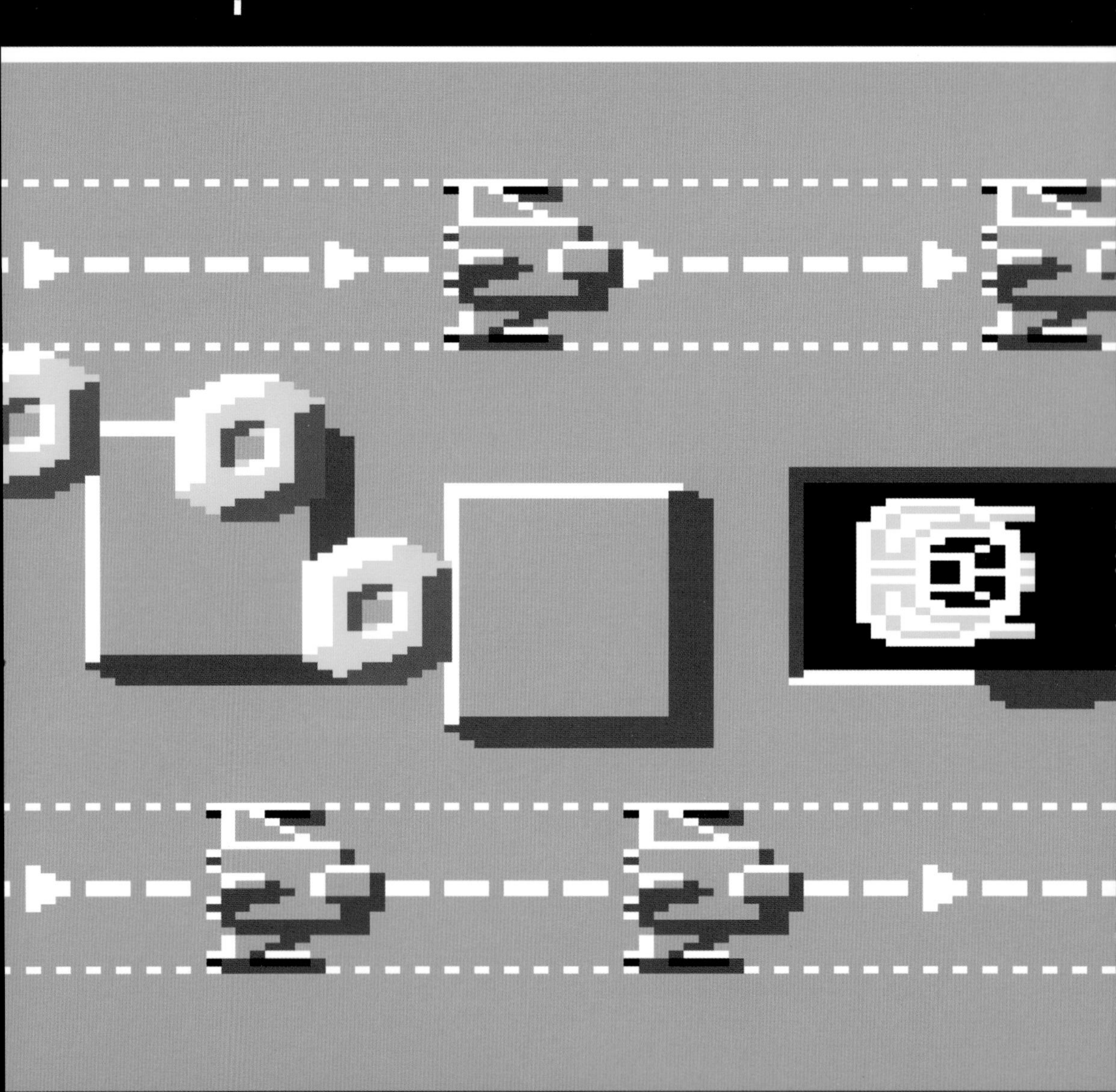

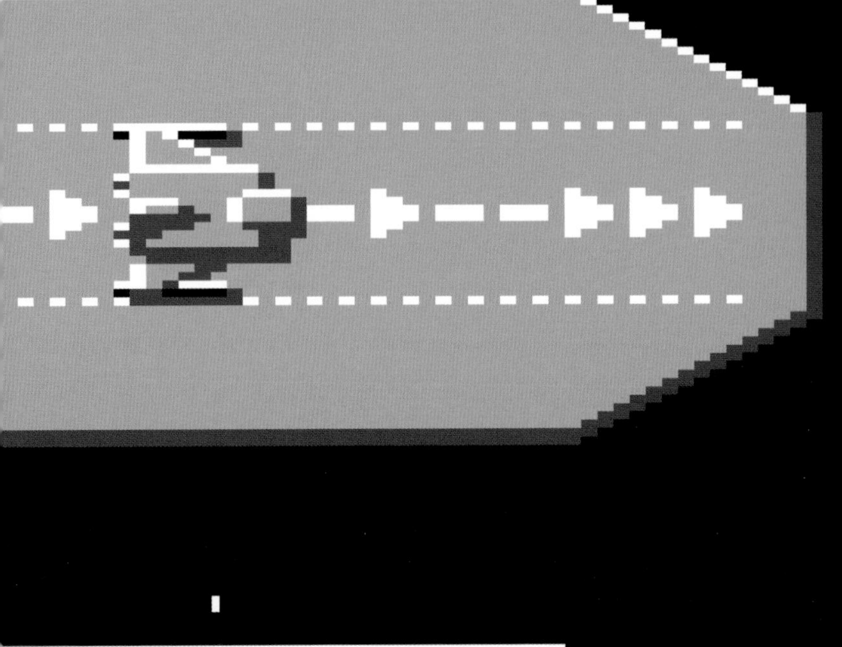

Uridium

"I knew Uridium was going to be UK number one before we even shipped it; such was the reception in the press. I'd stayed up all night helping to pack cassettes but the next evening I sank into the darkest feeling of despair. It had been a colossal effort and I just couldn't imagine how we could ever repeat it. The game was a total smash; probably Hewson's biggest ever hit, and had a big influence on our thinking for subsequent titles."

Andrew Hewson

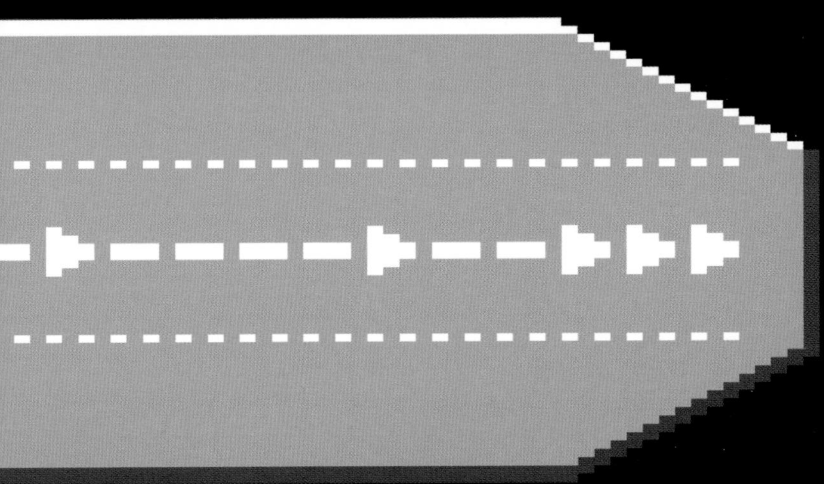

Released
1986

Genre
Scrolling shooter

Developer
Graftgold

Publisher
Hewson Consultants

The Pawn

"At the 1986 Novotel trade show in London when I was 18, I boldly proclaimed to the boss of Magnetic Scrolls that I could make The Pawn look just as good on C64 as it did on the ST and Amiga! She surprisingly said 'Prove it!' and we struck a deal a few days later. It required me to hand-pixel each of the 30 images from scratch as that was the only way to get close to the quality required. I was humbled and learnt a huge amount from that project."

Bob Stevenson

Released
1986

Genre
Text adventure

Developer
Magnetic Scrolls

Publisher
Rainbird

Rambo: First Blood Part II

"The size of the freely accessible play area is impressive. It's even possible to destroy houses and trees, and due to the opponent's superiority, a downright survival feeling sets in. Anyhow, Rambo always remained in the shadow of the similar shooter, Commando, since the gameplay was rather plain and frustrating at times, ending after ten minutes at the latest. Nevertheless, the atmosphere of the movie got captured skilfully, especially through the adaptation of the original soundtrack."

Oliver Lindau

Released
1986

Genre
Run and gun

Developer and Publisher
Ocean

RAMBO™

FIRST BLOOD™

PART II

ocean

Infiltrator

"One of many classic games that crossed the Atlantic courtesy of U.S. Gold, Infiltrator embodied the American movie culture of the 1980s by thrusting the player into an action adventure that could have easily been derived from a rejected Schwarzenegger script. In true action hero style, the player flies their helicopter to the enemy base and attempts to infiltrate various buildings and stop the 'Mad Leader'. Crisp graphics and an abundance of neat touches gave the player a genuine sense of stealth and suspense."

Andy Roberts

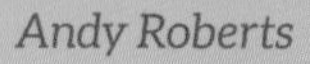

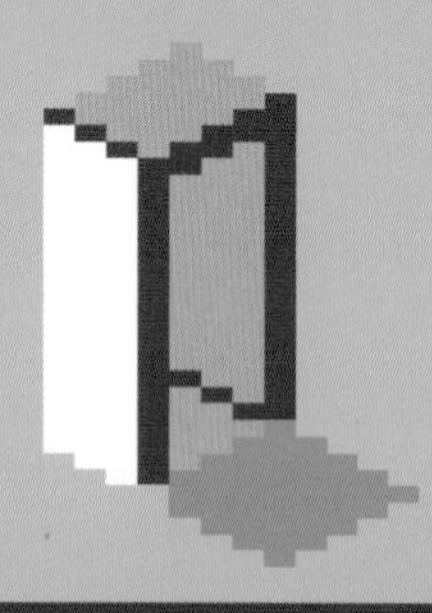

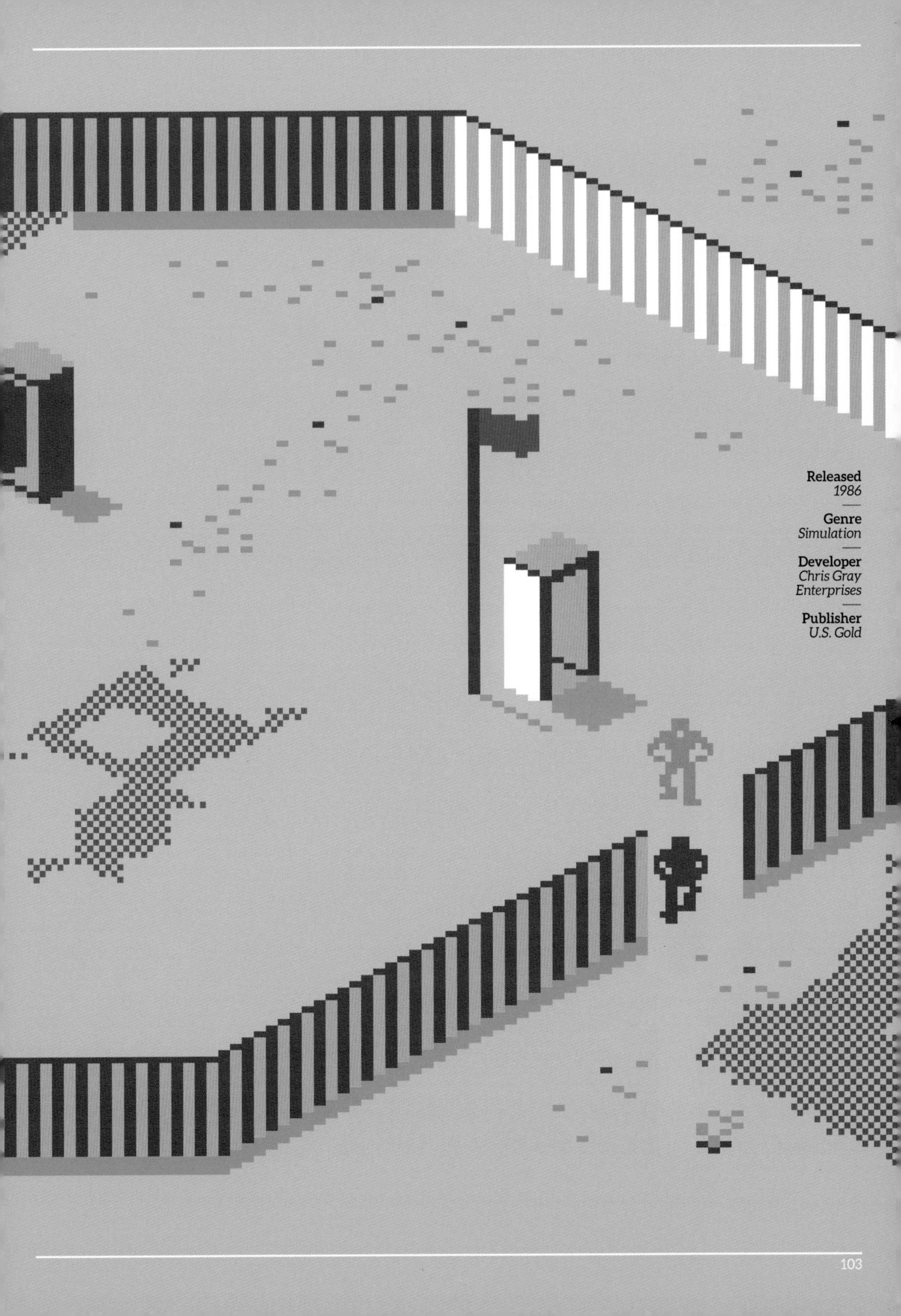

Released
1986

Genre
Simulation

Developer
Chris Gray Enterprises

Publisher
U.S. Gold

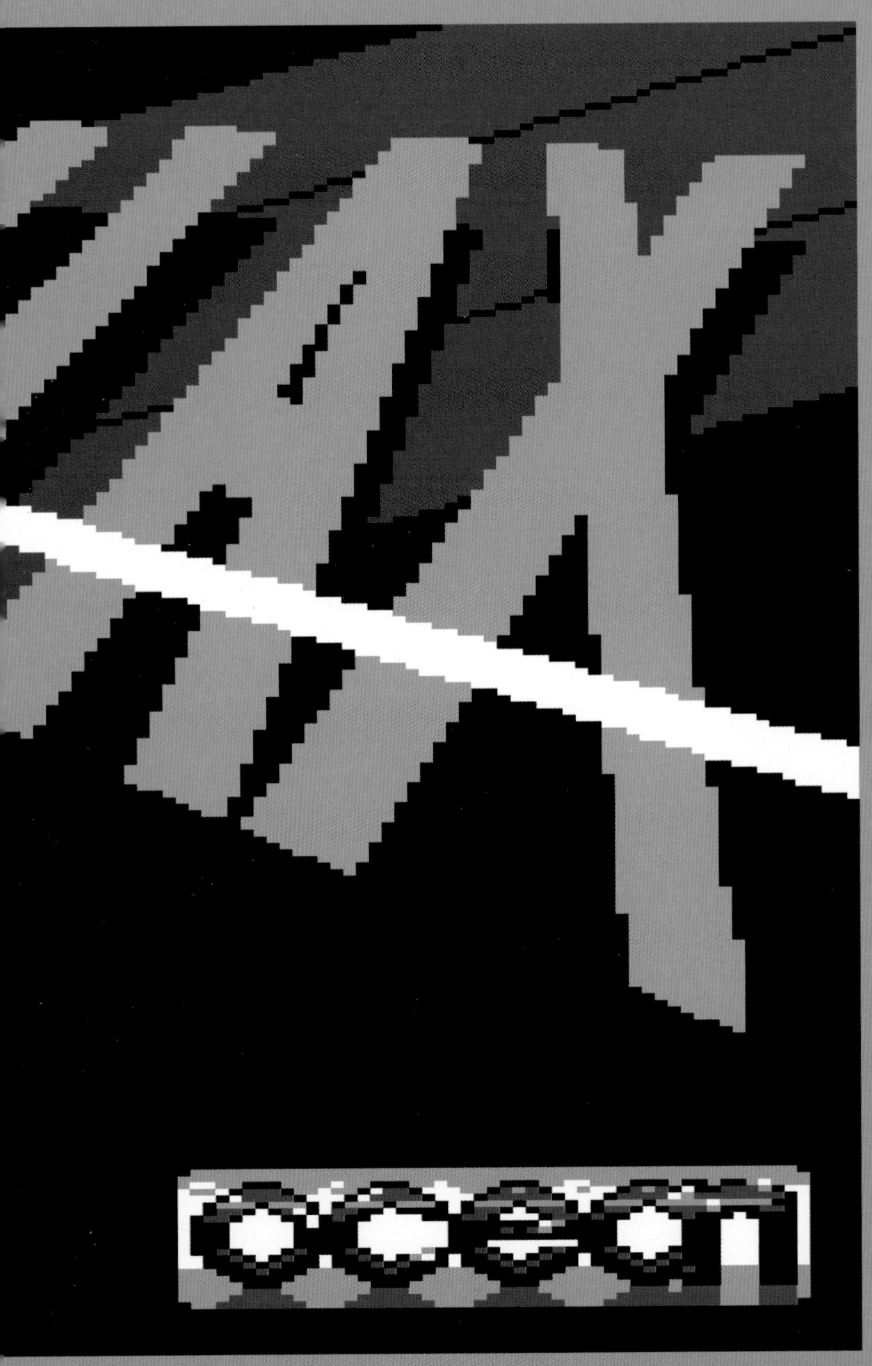

Parallax

"Parallax was our first game as Sensible Software. Signed up by Ocean in our first ever business meeting, we went home with a cheque for £1,000 and smoked cigars in the dinner carriage of the train on the way home to Essex... pity the royalty cheques never followed. The first time I heard Martin's music for this game the hairs stood up on the back of my neck – it was incredible. This was our lucky break."

Jon Hare

Released
1986

Genre
Scrolling shooter

Developer
Sensible Software

Publisher
Ocean

Thrust

"I'd been seduced by vector graphics coin-ops like Asteroids and Battlezone, and I loved the way they emulated real-world physics. So when Thrust appeared on the C64, I was totally blown away (not to mention it cost a measly two quid at the time). Rather than being restricted by the resolution of sprites or a game's clunky collision detection, Thrust's fluid control system allowed you to play with a remarkable level of freedom and precision. The levels may have been fiendishly designed but your biggest enemies were momentum, inertia and sheer blind panic."

Steve Jarratt

"Few games on the 64 made use of Newtonian mechanics – and even fewer as impressively as Thrust. Which makes the fact that this physics-fuelled fun was a budget release all the more WTF. Yes, Thrust smells like Atari's Gravitar but it's so much richer in flavour thanks to the inventive addition of spice: an orb to extract from each planet; a weighty orb attached by a rigid cable to your ship to radically affect its handling and make for some remarkable sphincter-clenching moments as you navigate the increasingly tight, twisty and deadly caverns."

Gary Penn

Released
1986

Genre
Arcade

Developer
Jeremy Smith

Publisher
Firebird

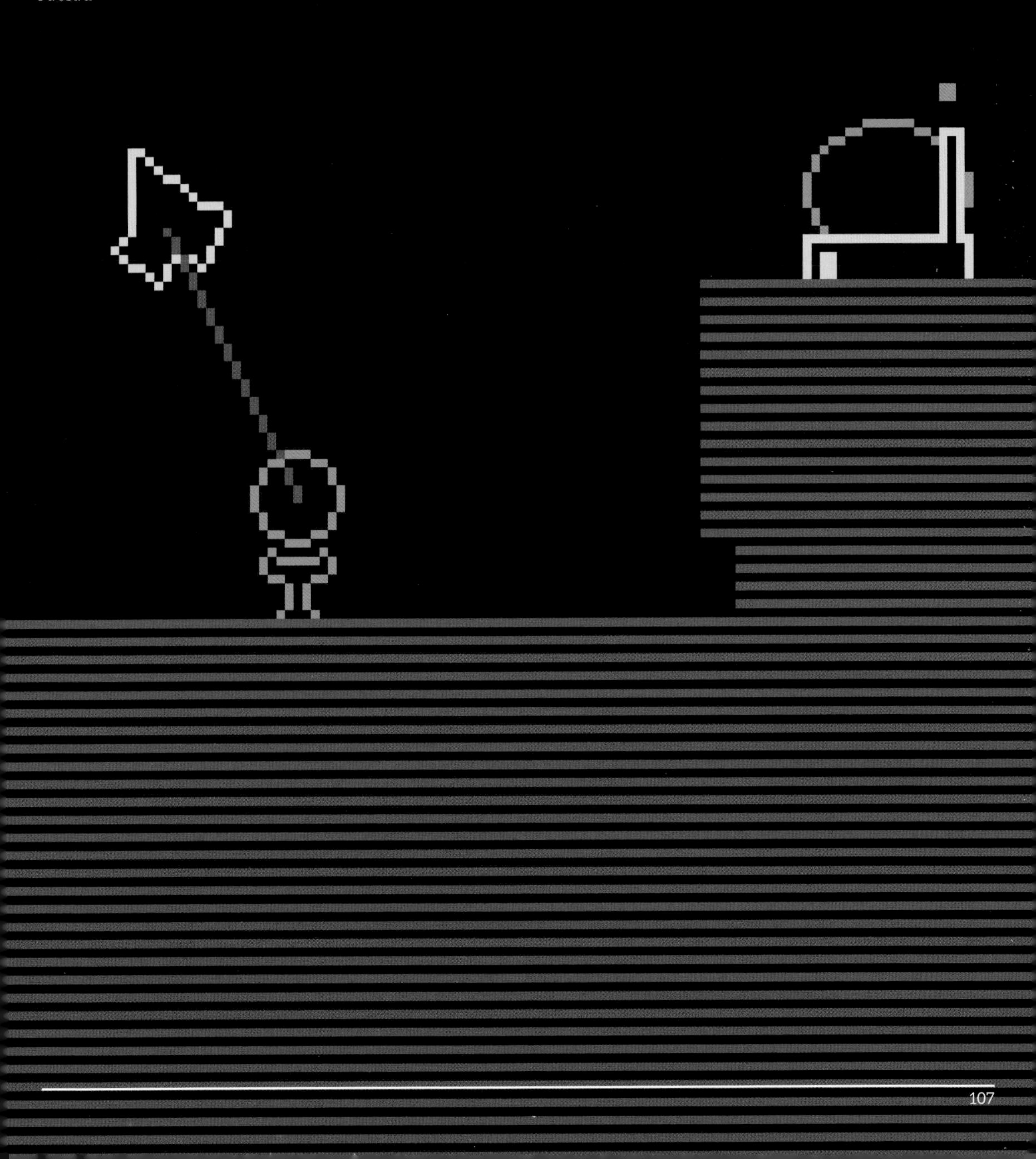

RESTORE
RETURN

> “The C64 punched above its weight on a number of levels, and it’s a real icon of ’80s culture.”
>
> *Stephen Ian Thomson, graphic artist*

Sanxion

"Thalamus had Bob Stevenson lined up to do the Sanxion loading screen but he couldn't commit to it as he was too busy doing other work. I knew Bob pretty well and on a few occasions he was kind enough to recommend me for work. The actual loading screen was an overnight job, I just copied the Oliver Frey artwork as best I could! Looking back on it now, it's pretty crude as I was still learning about pixelling at the time, but it's nice it's remembered fondly."

Mat Sneap

Released
1986

Genre
Scrolling shooter

Developer
Stavros Fasoulas

Publisher
Thalamus

Released
1986

Genre
Action puzzle

Developer and Publisher
Electric Dreams Software

Spindizzy

"Continuing my fascination with 3D graphics, Spindizzy immediately caught my attention for its angular Escher-like levels, and visual similarity to the Marble Madness coin-op. This flick-screen platform puzzler tasked you with exploring a vast network of mazes in control of a gyroscopic device called Gerald. Sadly the game's sensitive control system and overall difficulty meant I never got more than a few screens into the game's 400-plus areas! But that didn't stop me from returning to it, just to experience its unique visual style."

Steve Jarratt

The Sentinel

"The C64 played host to some extraordinary games, but one of the most innovative and atmospheric was The Sentinel. It delivered a tense game of cat and mouse, as you transported yourself around each abstract landscape in order to reach higher ground than that on which the Sentinel stood. Absorb the landscape's custodian, and you moved on to the next level. As one of the first fully polygonal 3D games, it was a standout in its day, and the unhurried speed of the camera only served to make the game even more suspenseful. If someone updated this for the iPad, I'd buy a copy tomorrow."

Steve Jarratt

Released
1986

Genre
Strategy

Developer
Geoff Crammond

Publisher
Firebird

Rainbow Islands *Graftgold*

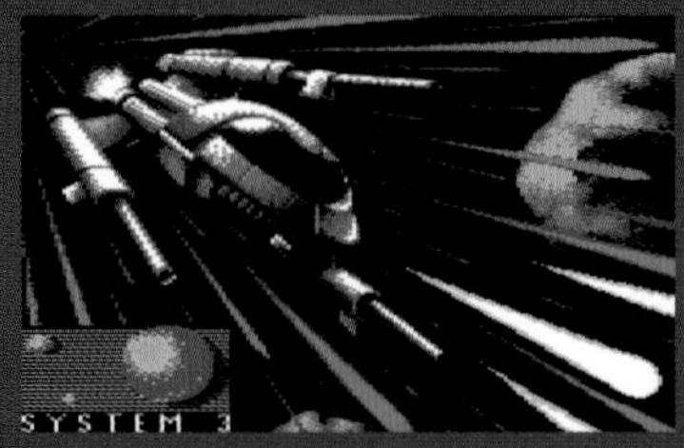

Dominator *System 3*

Time Machine *Vivid Image*

Firefly *Special FX*

Stormlord *Hewson Consultants*

Warhawk *Proteus Developments*

Short Circuit *Ocean*

Tetris *Andromeda Software*

Game Over *Dinamic*

Turrican *Rainbow Arts*

Arkanoid *Imagine*

Solomon's Key *Probe Software*

Iron Lord *Ubi Soft*

Treasure Island Dizzy *Codemasters*

R-Type *Rainbow Arts*

Brave Starr *Probe Software*

Batman: The Caped Crusader *Special FX*

BMX Kidz *Firebird*

Soul Crystal *Starbyte Software*

Cobra *Ocean*

Star Wars *Vektor Grafix*

Miami Vice *Ocean*

Space Harrier *Elite Systems*

Head Over Heels *Ocean*

Kane *Mastertronic*

Green Beret *Imagine*

Cybernoid II *Hewson Consultants*

Retrograde *Apex Computer Productions*

Rastan *Imagine*

The Last V8 *Mastertronic*

The Staff of Karnath *Ultimate*

Druid II *Electralyte*

Phobia *Image Works*

Platoon *Ocean*

Robin of the Wood *Odin Computer Graphics*

Ghouls 'n Ghosts *Software Creations*

Gunship

"When Microprose released Gunship in 1986, military airborne warfare was hip. Kids loved action movies like Iron Eagle and Top Gun with iconic pilots and high-tech aircraft. The AH-64 Apache was just introduced by the US Military and Microprose made it possible to operate this state of the art combat helicopter at home! As you would expect from Microprose the attention to detail was incredible and the package content very comprehensive. Gunship truly set new benchmarks."

Rocco Di Leo

SHIP

Released
1986

Genre
Simulation

Developer and Publisher
Microprose Software

Buggy Boy

"Never judge a book by its cover. At first sight, Buggy Boy looks like a simple obstacle racing game with rough, bulky graphics and sound which would rather fit a slot machine. The gameplay, however, is particularly fluent and the race tracks are built brilliantly. The carefully placed bonus flags, time bonuses and jumps tempt the player to try risky manoeuvres again and again, which means it's the player themselves causing the level of difficulty in this incredibly addictive game."

Oliver Lindau

Released
1987

Genre
Racing

Developer
Bob and Dave Thomas

Publisher
Elite Systems

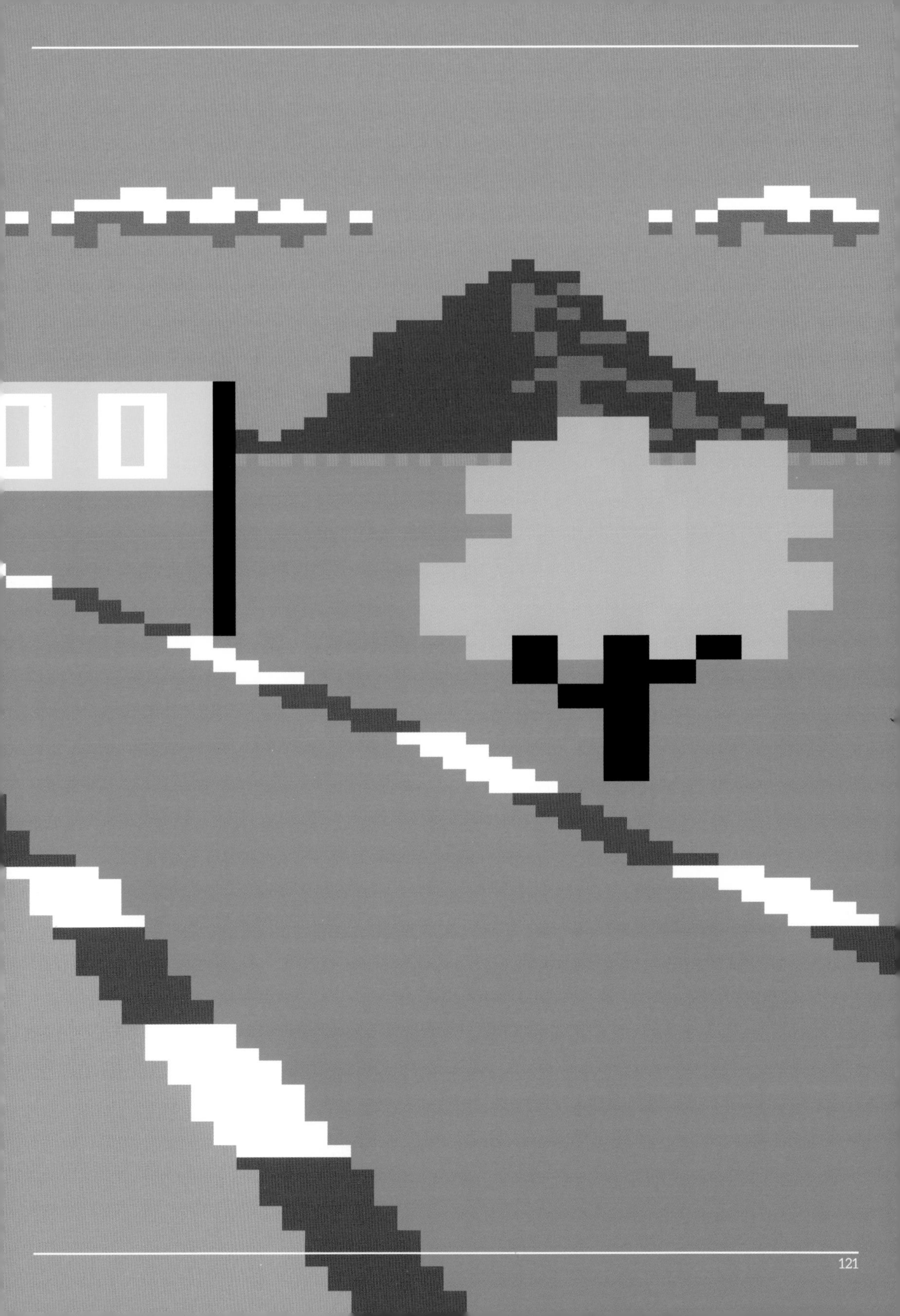

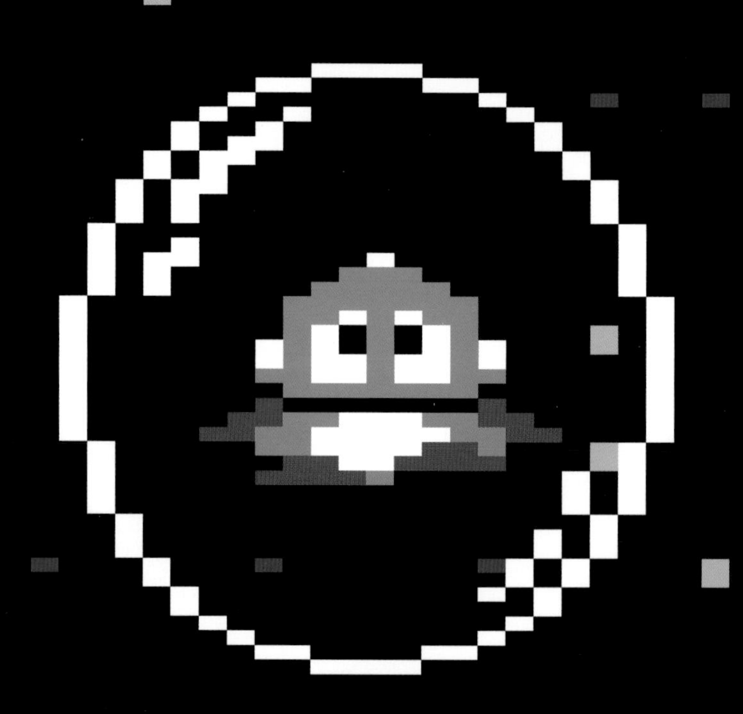

Bubble Bobble

"Bubble Bobble was just such a fantastic arcade game that to get anywhere near the playability of the original would make a good C64 game. Typical of the time, the conversion took around three months. I was very happy that we managed to get all the levels in although we did have to lose some presentation content and some sprite images."

Stephen Ruddy

Released
1987

Genre
Platformer

Developers
Software Creations

Publisher
Firebird

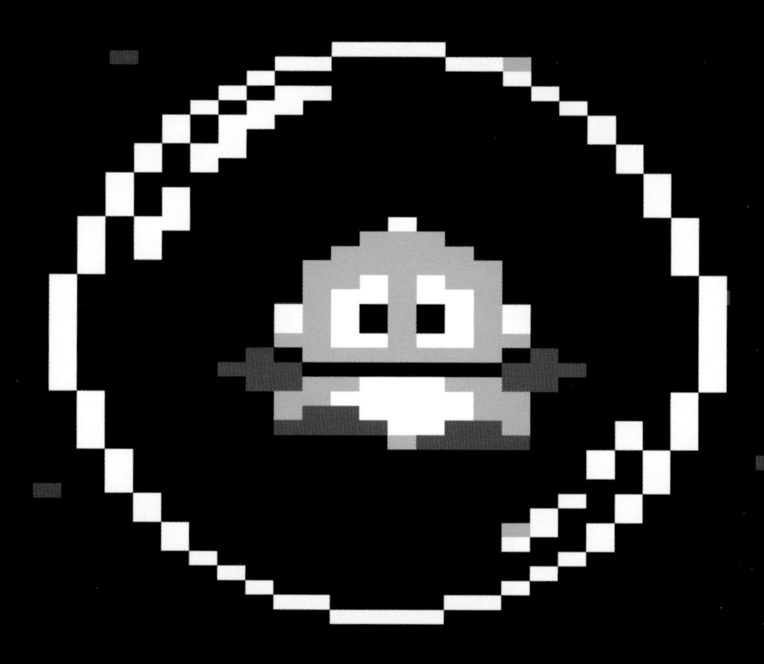

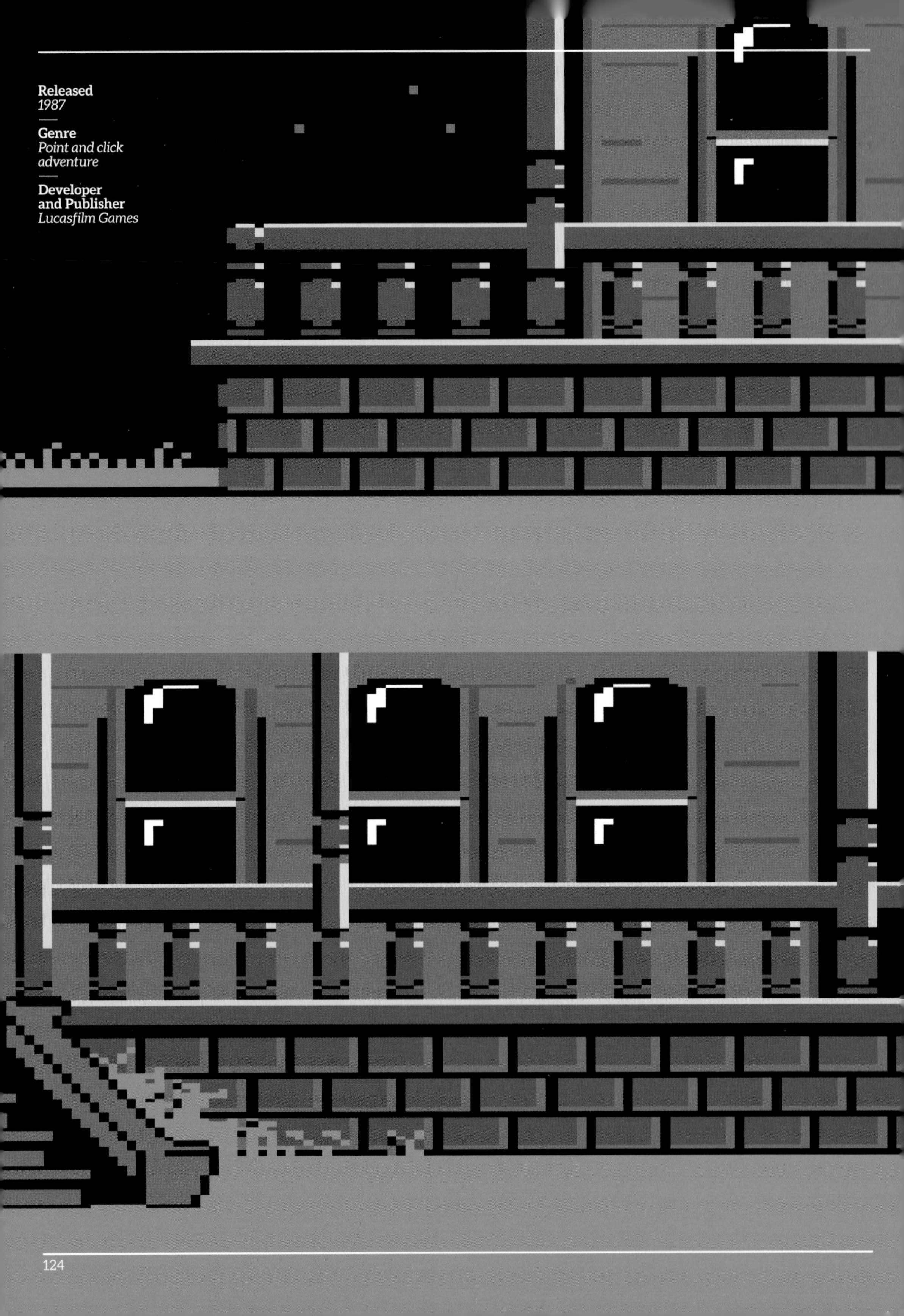

Released
1987

Genre
Point and click adventure

Developer and Publisher
Lucasfilm Games

Maniac Mansion

"The Commodore 64 is quite possibly the greatest computer ever built and Maniac Mansion would not exist without it. Its combination of simplicity, sophistication and limitations provided the perfect storm of creative and technical innovation that allowed Maniac Mansion to go on to define the point-and-click genre. It was a joy and wonder to program and will forever remain my favourite computer."

Ron Gilbert

The Last Ninja

I saw an image where a ninja fighter blended in with a dark background and it was then that I recognised that the eyes surrounded by the black of the mask immediately conveys 'ninja' without any more information needed. I used a mirror to study my own eyes as reference and utilised a small pipette to put water drops on my forehead to get the look of beads of sweat. In those early days of video games I was using paints, inks and airbrushes to create artwork."

Steinar Lund

Releas
19

Gen
Action adventu

**Develop
and Publish**
System

efender
f the Crown

h, Defender of the
rown. How I loved
our visual splendour.
his was a game that
red my imagination
nd forced me to believe
nat games could be epic,
inematic and important.
Jnfortunately it was
cuppered by cripplingly
ow loading tapes. Fancy
60-second sword fight?
Vait a couple of mins.
nvade a neighbouring
ingdom? You might
ave to wait another
en minutes. How
vell have you done?
Jo fricking idea, I went
nd had a cider down
he skateboard park
alf an hour ago.
great idea conceived
oo early, perhaps."

ndy Dyer

eleased
987

enre
trategy

evelopers
Aaster Designer
oftware

ublisher
Cinemaware

IK+

"Sometimes games just come together; they have everything. For a fighting game of the '80s IK+ was one of them. It had the awesome soundtrack by the legendary Rob Hubbard and an animation and fighting system that Archer MacLean made worth mastering – and timing was everything. As a young gamer becoming the very best at this was crucial, as two-player mode was great fun (almost as much as the cheats available). Drop your pants in an instant!"

GamesYouLoved

Released
1987

Genre
Fighting

Developer
Archer MacLean

Publisher
System 3

Released
1987

Genre
Scrolling shooter

Developer
Martin Walker

Publisher
Thalamus

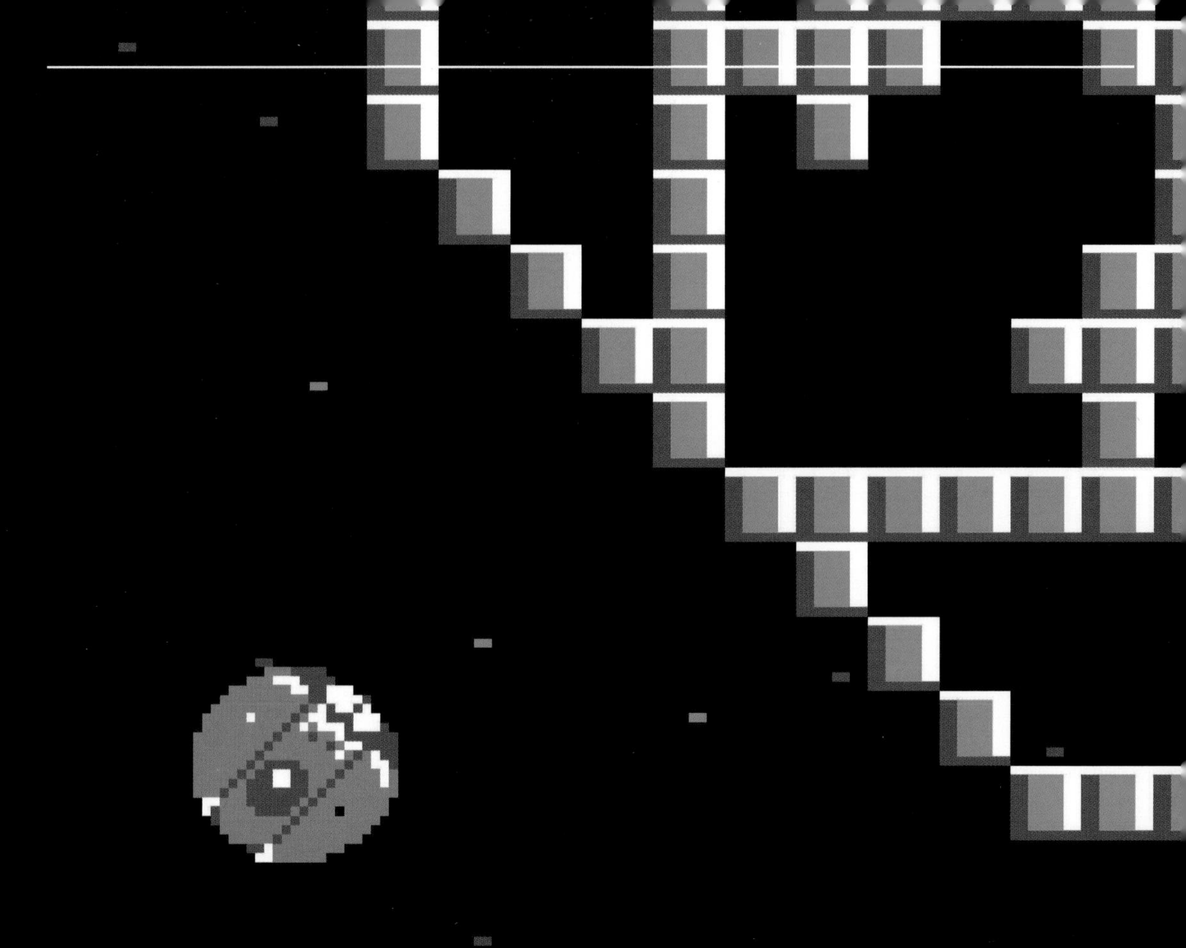

Hunter's Moon

"Hunter's Moon was a joy to create, but I was particularly pleased with my 'computerised Spirograph' approach to level creation, which managed to cram a massive 128 different levels into very limited memory. Each level had eight worker cells, in different start positions and pointing in different directions, and then they were given instructions to travel a specific distance, then to turn by a specific angle, and repeat the process indefinitely to create the hive structures. Easy when you know how!"

Martin Walker

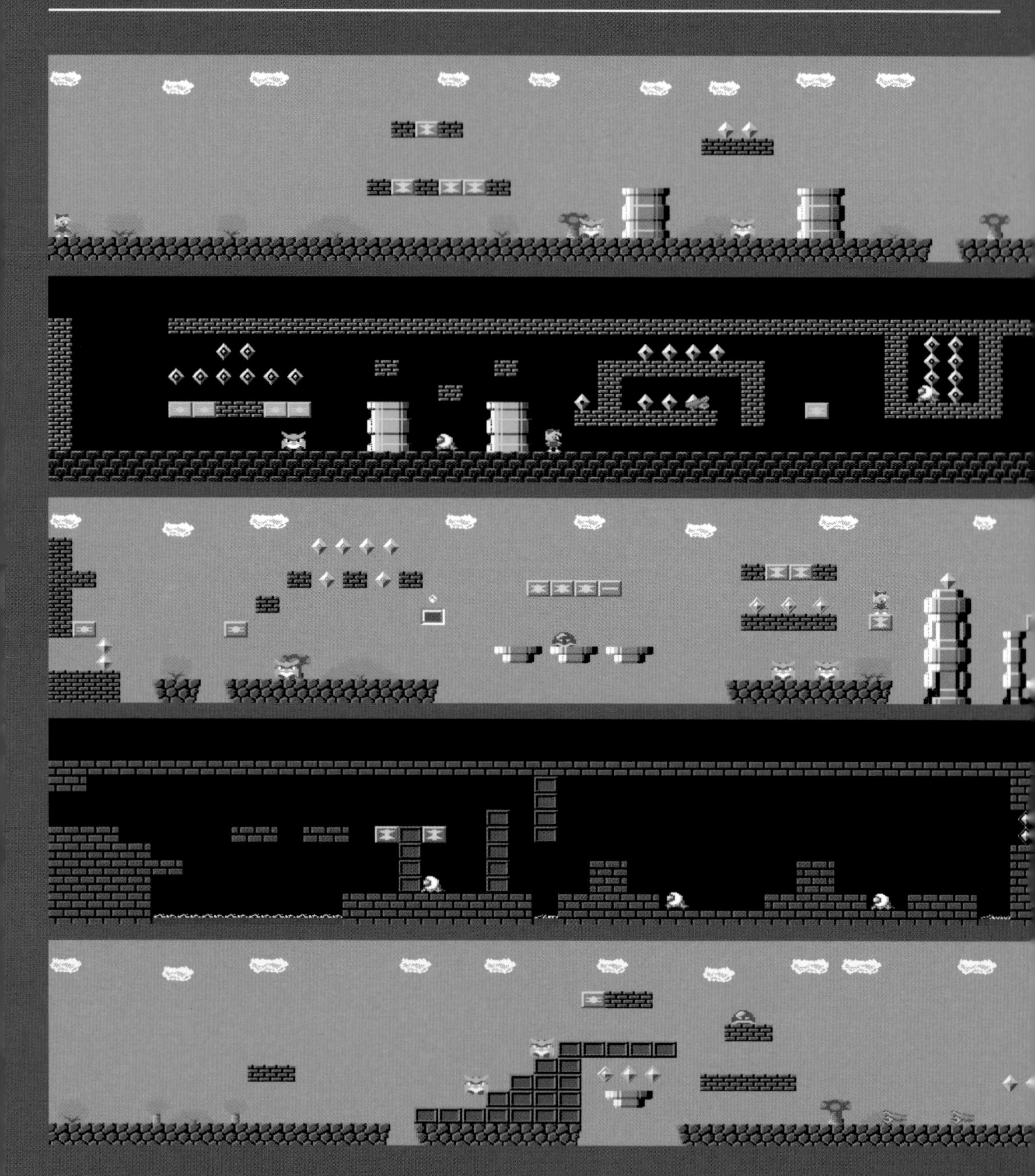

The Great Giana Sisters

"When I first saw The Great Giana Sisters running on a Commodore 64 it completely blew my mind, and it was the first game I played from beginning to the end. For me this was the first platform, jump and run game ever! In addition to the more-or-less simple graphics, the sound from audio magician Chris Hülsbeck made the game a great experience. Only later when I saw Super Mario for the first time did I realise that Giana Sisters looked somehow similar..."

Luca Argentiero

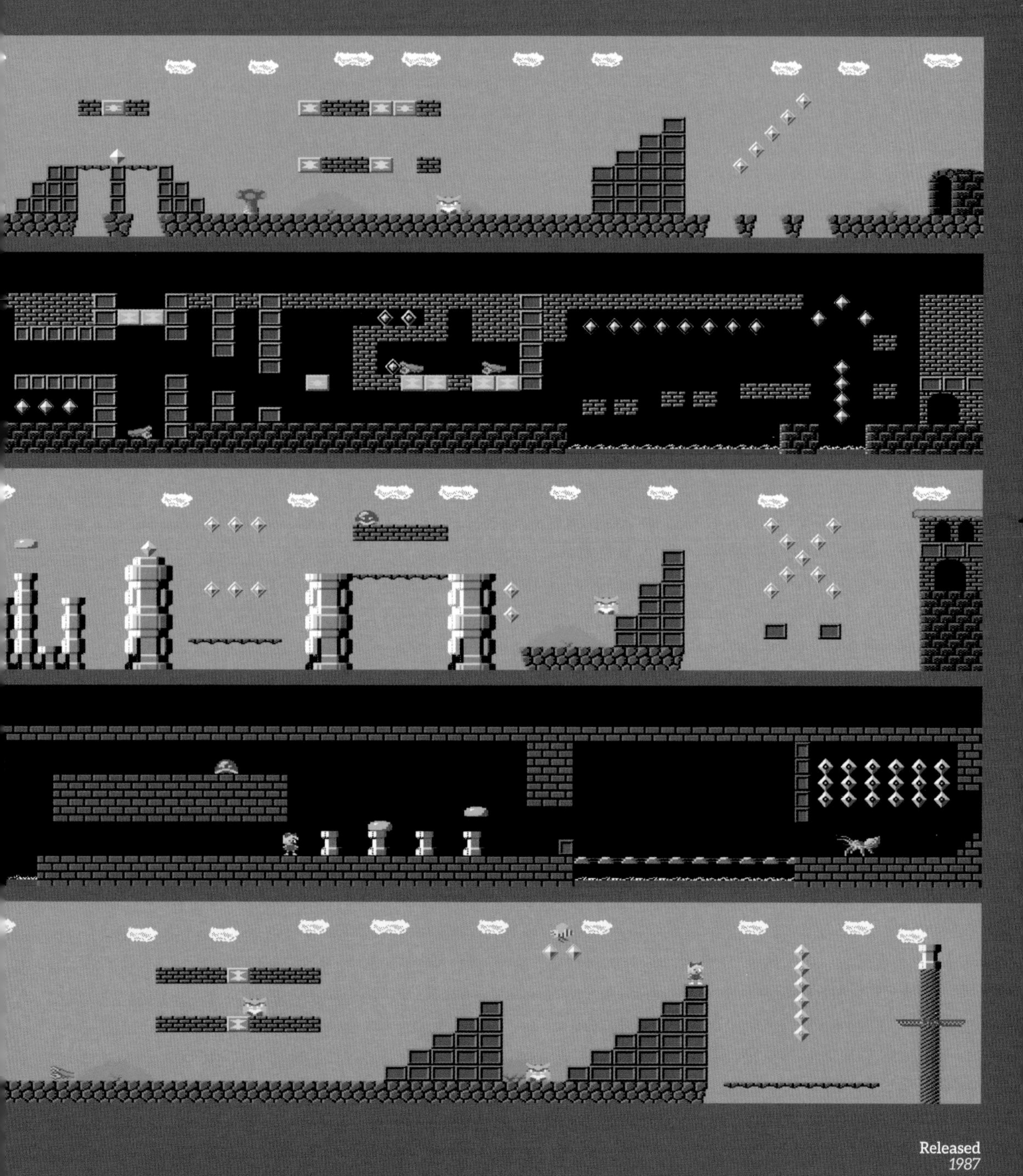

Released
1987

Genre
Platformer

Developer
Time Warp Productions

Publisher
Rainbow Arts

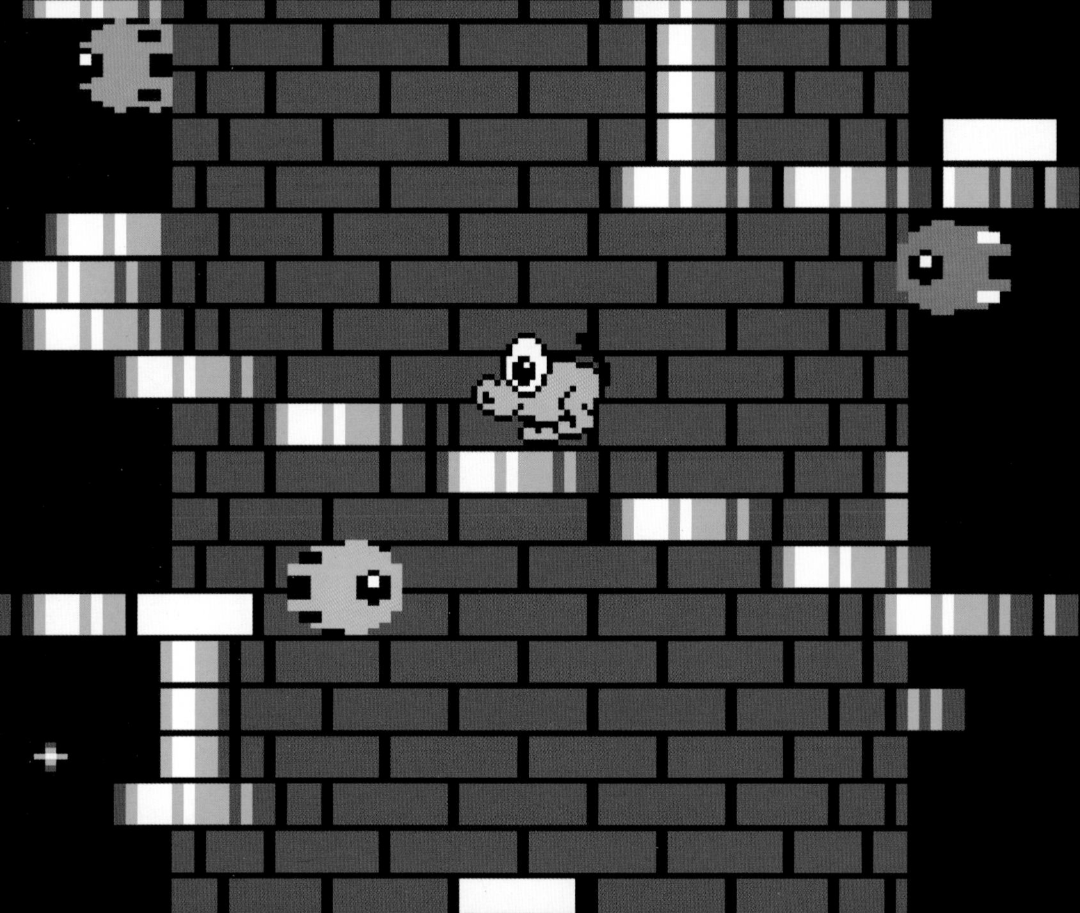

Platoon

Released
1987

Genre
Action

Developer and Publisher
Ocean

Artwork
Oliver Frey

Shoot-'Em-Up Construction Kit

Released
1987

Genre
Utlity

Developer
Sensible Software

Publisher
Outlaw Productions

Artwork
Oliver Frey

Released
1987

Genre
Scrolling shooter

Developer
Sensible Software

Publisher
Ocean

Wizball

"This 'Game of the Decade' was Inspired by Dropzone and Nemesis. One day I got to Chris's house and he showed me this weird bouncing ball control he'd invented. I drew a stupid grinning green head and Wizball was born. Chris added loads of weapons and I came up with the landscape colouring idea so we added paint bubbles to catch. The paint collecting orbiting satellite SFX sounded like 'meows' so we called it 'catellite'."

Jon Hare

Que-Dex

Flesh tones were always tricky on the C64 but that never stopped me from trying. The irony that I was drawing a hand holding a joystick by hand using a joystick was not lost on me! Almost all the graphics I created on the C64 were with Paint Magic and a Kempston Competition Pro joystick. It was the daftest and most laborious technique for creating graphics, but on the C64 I never did it any other way."

Paul Docherty

Released
1987

Genre
Action puzzle

Developer
Stavros Fasoulas

Publisher
Thalamus

Driller

"As a haunting theme with echoes of Hallowe'en and Phantom of the Opera infiltrates your ears, the sheer vastness of the task ahead is matched with the blackness of the sky, punctuated by some really good looking solid graphics. It's a pity they move so slowly, although that's something emulation has 'fixed' since. Driller was the first use of the Freescape engine, and future games would improve on the bar set by this release."

Mat Allen

Released
1987

Genre
Puzzle adventure

Developer
Major Developments

Publisher
Incentive Software

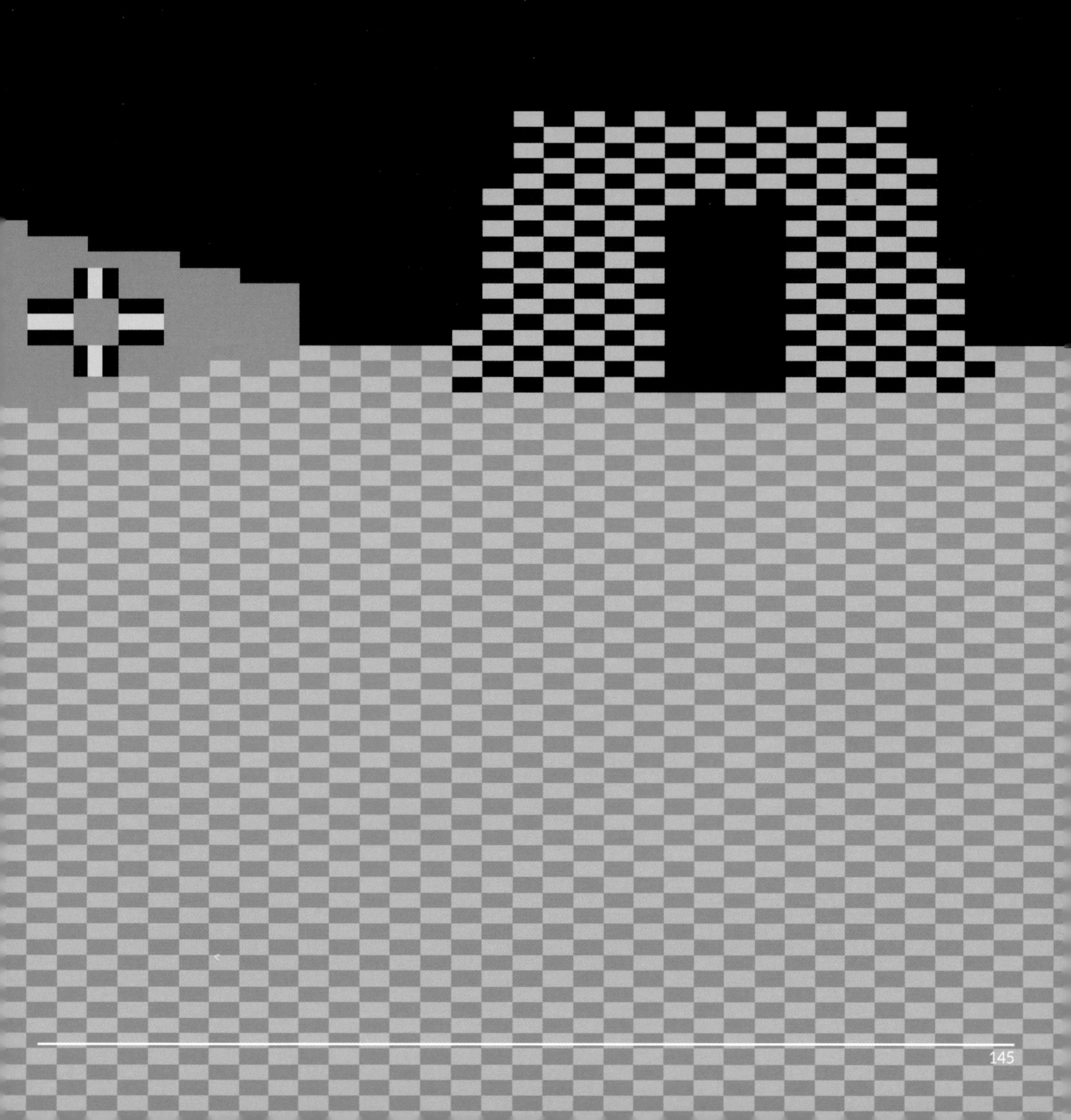

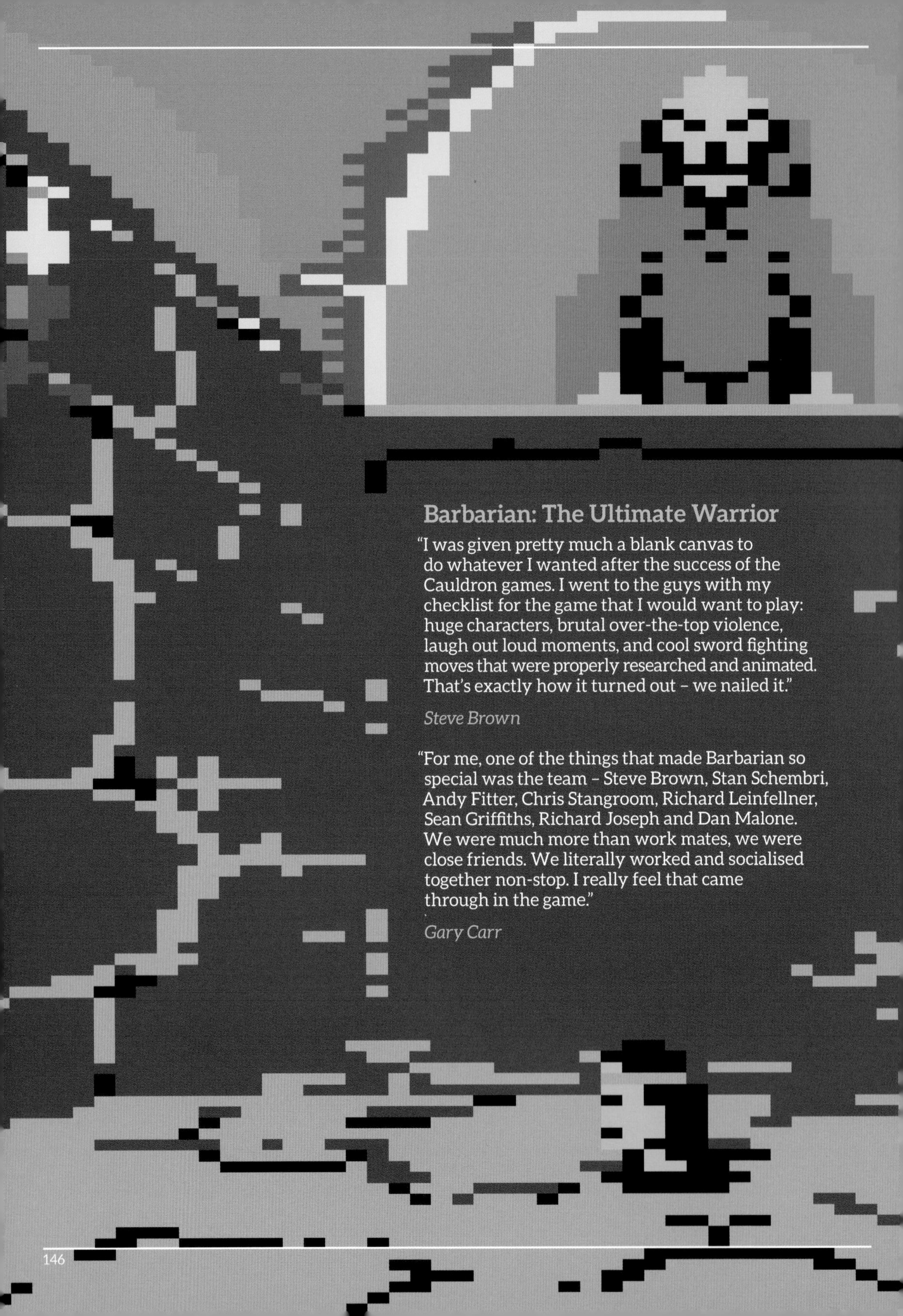

Barbarian: The Ultimate Warrior

"I was given pretty much a blank canvas to do whatever I wanted after the success of the Cauldron games. I went to the guys with my checklist for the game that I would want to play: huge characters, brutal over-the-top violence, laugh out loud moments, and cool sword fighting moves that were properly researched and animated. That's exactly how it turned out – we nailed it."

Steve Brown

"For me, one of the things that made Barbarian so special was the team – Steve Brown, Stan Schembri, Andy Fitter, Chris Stangroom, Richard Leinfellner, Sean Griffiths, Richard Joseph and Dan Malone. We were much more than work mates, we were close friends. We literally worked and socialised together non-stop. I really feel that came through in the game."

Gary Carr

Released
1987

Genre
Fighting

Developer and Publisher
Palace Software

Released *1987* / Genre *Sports* / Developer and Publisher *Codemasters*

Grand Prix Simulator

"A dynamic loading screen harking back to the early '80s and the Ferrari and McClaren clashes in F1. Based on the box art, the game was a Supersprint style one with what looked like small coloured shoe boxes for cars as I recall. The loading screens were intended to sell the budget games."

Steven Day

Released *1987* / Genre *Sports* / Developer *Digital Persuasion* / Publisher *Codemasters*

ATV Simulator

"Probably my favourite of the Codemasters screens I did. I also converted the background graphics for the game as I recall, as a rush job with both being completed inside two days when another artist failed to deliver on time. As a general guide most of my loading screens were completed in the eight-to-ten-hour hour mark in order to make them commercially viable."

Steven Day

Released *1988* / **Genre** *Sports* / **Developer and Publisher** *Codemasters*

Professional BMX Simulator

"This was one of a pair of screens done for the flagship game of a slightly more expensive range of Codemasters releases. When doing this screen I used a few elements from Jim Wilson's original BMX Simulator loading screen in order to preserve brand continuity. My original screen read 'Super BMX Simulator' which were changed in-house to 'Professional' later (badly)."

Steven Day

Released *1988* / **Genre** *Sports* / **Developer** *Arcana Software Design* / **Publisher** *Codemasters*

Professional Snooker Simulator

"Generally, loading screens were based upon the cassette inlay artwork but an exception in this case was Pro Snooker. It was my very first commissioned loading screen, and was requested to be original artwork, as the cassette inlay was not popular at Codemasters. The player as I recall was an '80s snooker player named Doug Mountjoy."

Steven Day

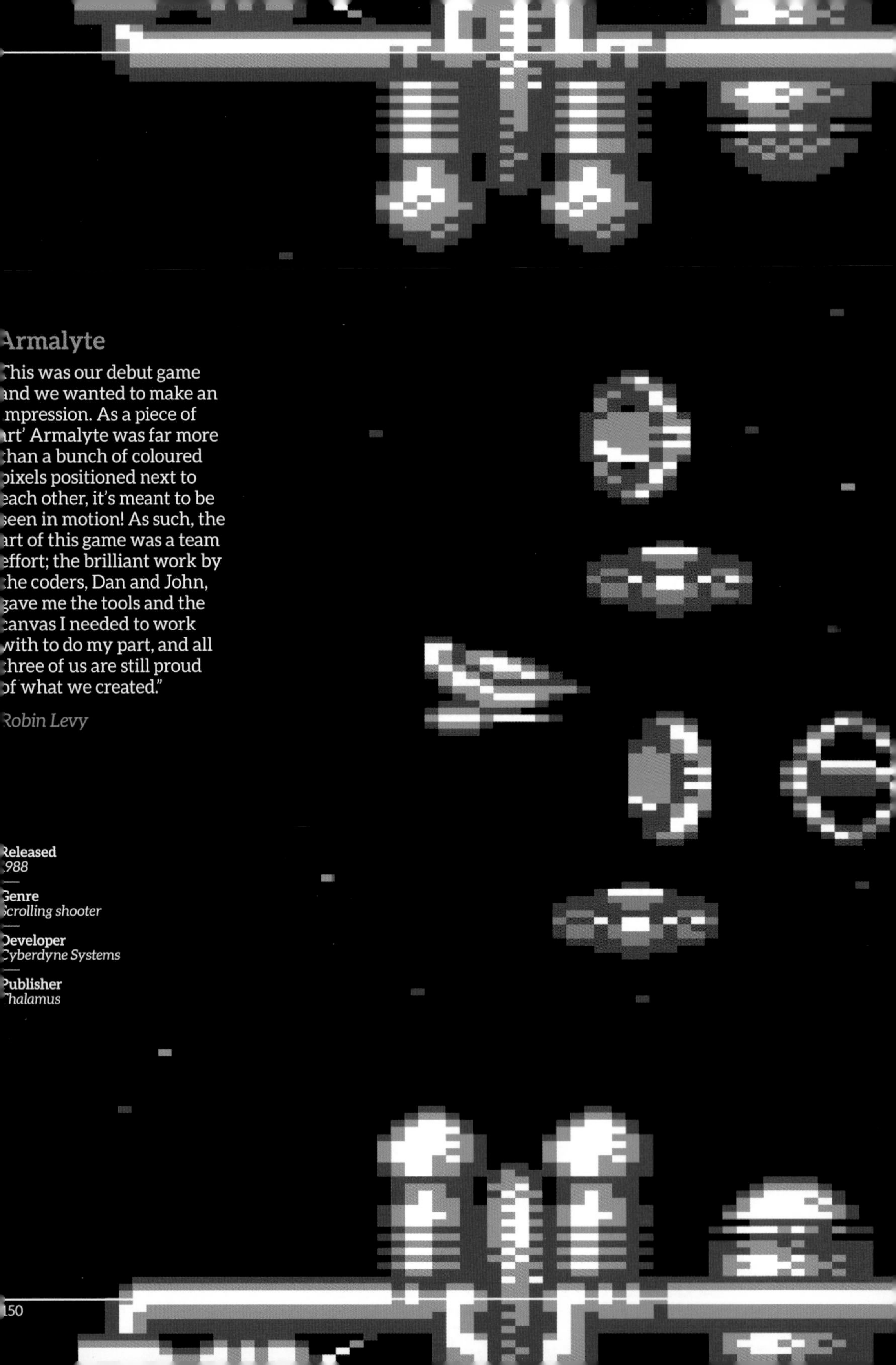

Armalyte

This was our debut game and we wanted to make an impression. As a piece of 'art' Armalyte was far more than a bunch of coloured pixels positioned next to each other, it's meant to be seen in motion! As such, the art of this game was a team effort; the brilliant work by the coders, Dan and John, gave me the tools and the canvas I needed to work with to do my part, and all three of us are still proud of what we created."

Robin Levy

Released
1988

Genre
Scrolling shooter

Developer
Cyberdyne Systems

Publisher
Thalamus

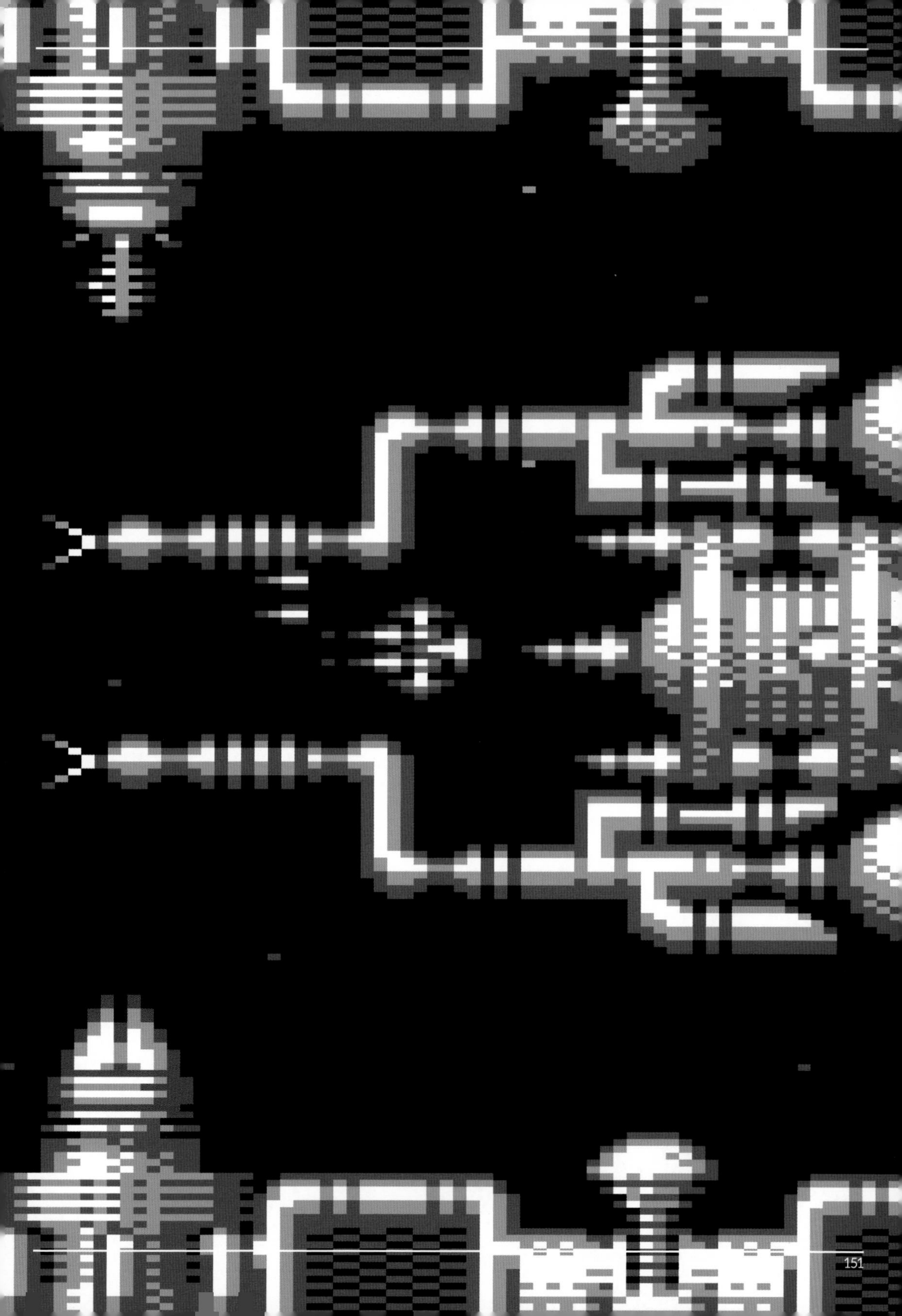

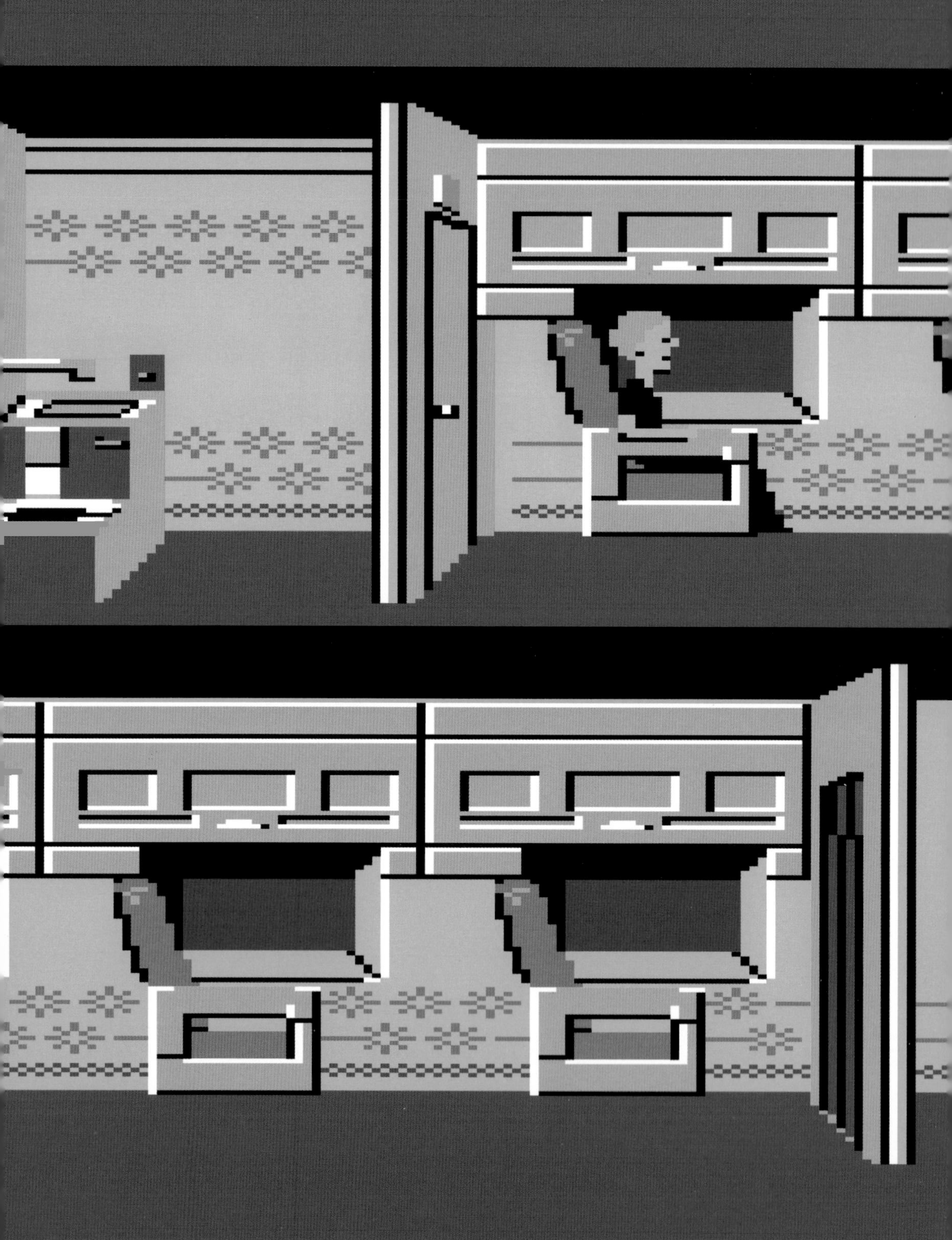

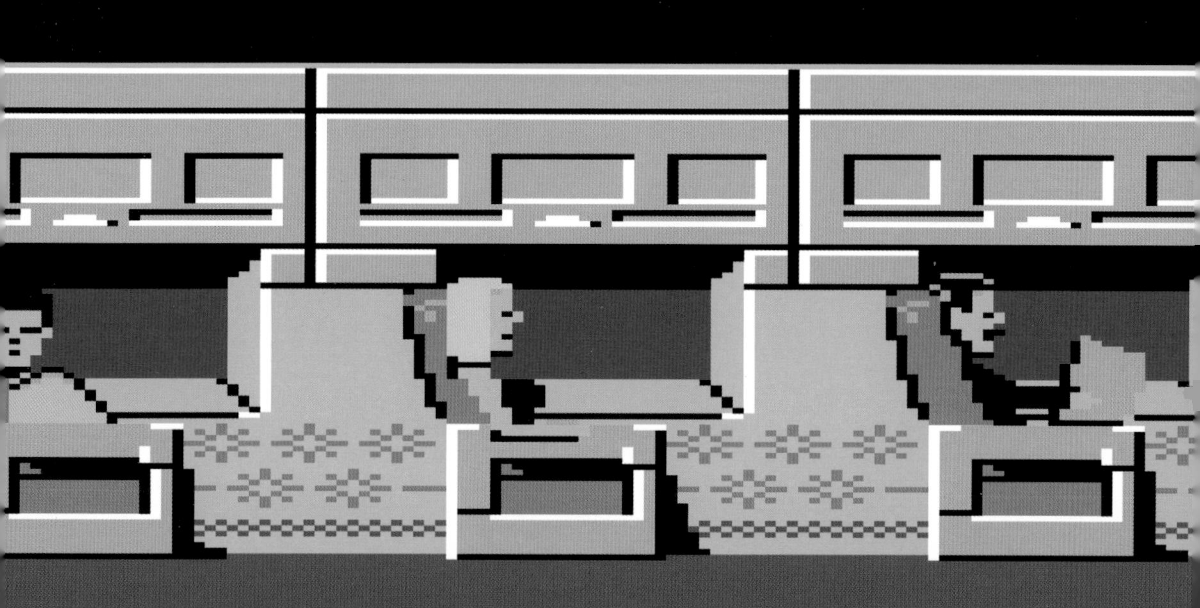

Zak McKracken and the Alien Mindbenders

"A fish in a bowl, a loaf of bread, and a Groucho Marx disguise. Just a few of the items you'll need during this highly enjoyable successor to Maniac Mansion, where your task is to prevent aliens taking over the Earth using a 60Hz hum. It retained all the same visual and aesthetic charm, and lumped on a substantial dash of wit, sarcasm and subtle humour for good measure. Don't forget the airport codes…"

Mat Allen

Released
1988

Genre
Point and click adventure

Developer and Publisher
Lucasfilm Games

Cybernoid

Cybernoid was Raffaele Cecco's second title for us and it was technically superb with lots of effects being thrown around on screen. As a result many people credited the game for helping to extend the life of the 8-bit machines with 16-bit looming on the horizon. We always believed in promoting the creators of our games and Cybernoid certainly cemented Raffaele as something of a star."

Andrew Hewson

The loading screen was based on the box artwork. I found it easier to turn the box upside down and draw the ship that way, then rotate it to the right orientation! The logo and planet were drawn separately, and the ship composited on top using a nifty feature of the Koala Painter touch tablet."

Stephen Robertson

Released *1988* / **Genre** *Flick screen shooter* / **Developer** *Raffaele Cecco* / **Publisher** *Hewson Consultants*

Last Ninja 2

"Last Ninja 2 built on the template we created for the original. The Integrator allowed me to overlay and assemble chunks of multi-colour art that I made using a mouse. The isometric 1:2 angle was unusual and challenging to animate. We didn't multiplex the sprites so the ninja and his opponents shared the same torso and legs, with another sprite for the weapon and a 1 sprite colour overlay for the face, hands and enemy outfits. A shadow was also added to the characters in this sequel."

Hugh Riley

Released
1988

Genre
Action adventure

Developer and Publisher
System 3

> "Painting in pixels was never more magical for me than when I was sitting in a darkened room with just a joystick hooked up to the C64 and the cathode ray tube glowing in front of me."

Paul Docherty, graphic artist

Hawkeye

Hawkeye was strongly influenced by arcade game Rygar (which Mario could finish in the arcades with just one guilder!). We did something which had never been done before: a multilayer parallax scroller which was held to be impossible until then on the C64. The music is by the then unknown 14-year-old Jeroen Tel who we introduced to the industry. It took nearly two years to build but was all worth it in the end as it won a gold medal award in Zzap!64."

Jacco Van 't Riet

Released
1988

Genre
Run and gun

Developer
Boys Without Brains

Publisher
Thalamus

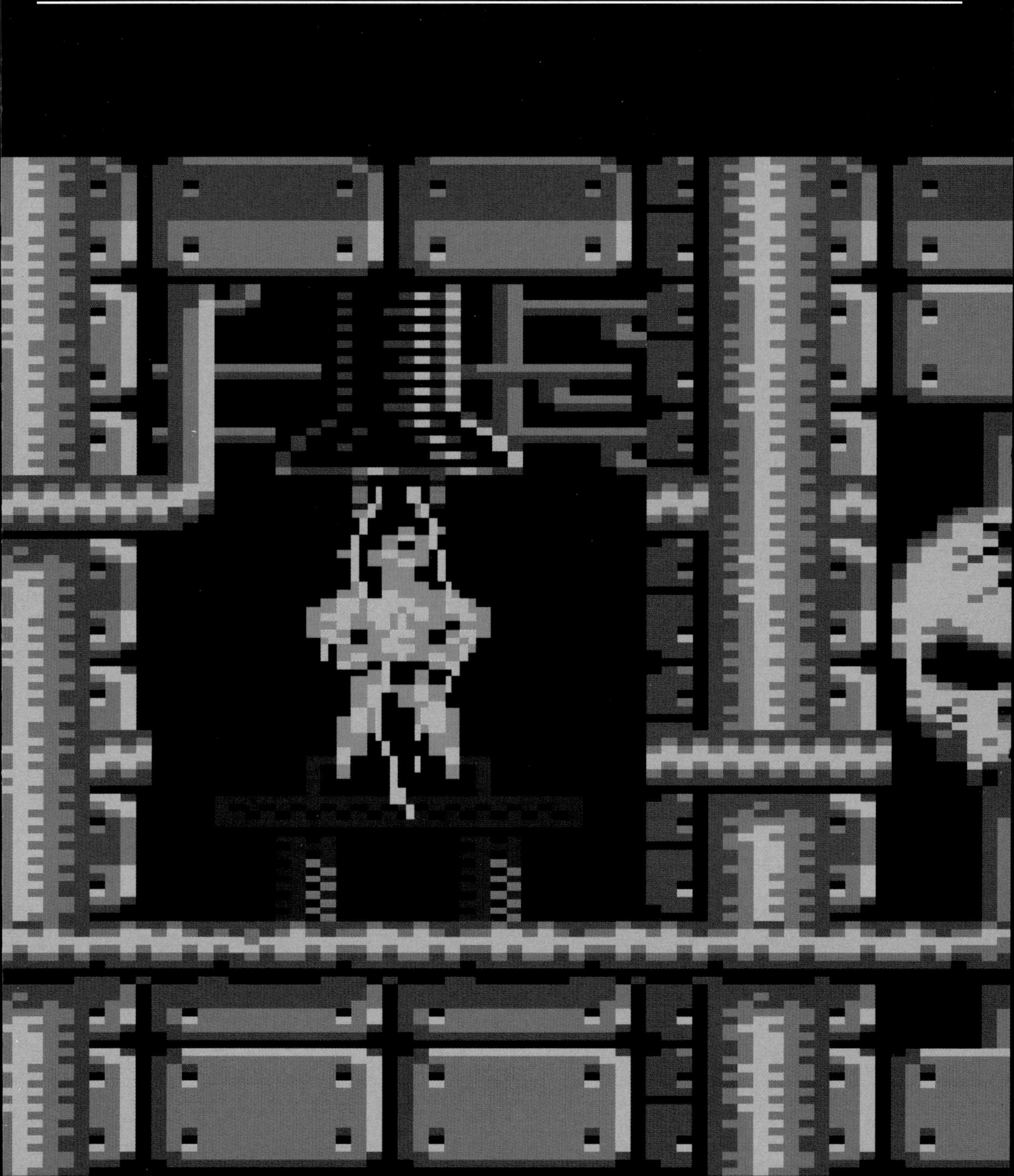

WEC Le Mans

Released
1988

Genre
Racing

Developer and Publisher
Imagine

Artwork
Oliver Frey

Katakis

Released
1988

Genre
Scrolling shooter

Developer
Manfred Trenz

Publisher
Rainbow Arts

Artwork
Oliver Frey

Batman
The Movie

"In 1989 you couldn't miss the Batman phenomenon. The hype was incredible. Around the film came Ocean's adaptation which, despite being multi-load, was an enjoyable romp through Gotham City. A nice soundtrack to accompany good graphics and simple but addictive gameplay, it was assured success and is still playable today."

Robin Hogg

Released
1989

Genre
Action

Developer and Publisher
Ocean

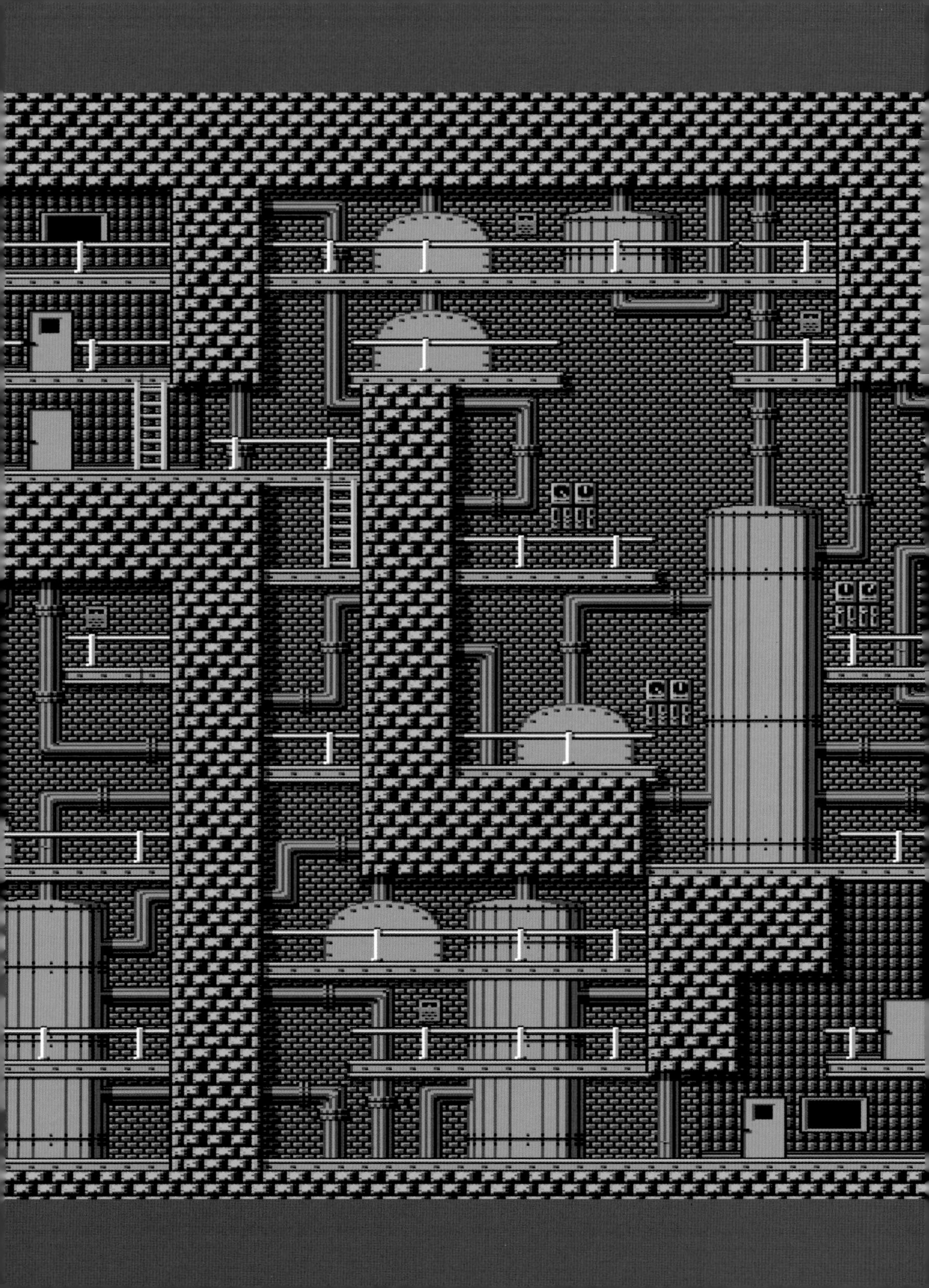

MYTH: History in the Making

"This was one of my favourite games that I helped create and make. It was based on a paper design that System 3 approached Peter Baron and myself to do. Pete and I had a very improvisational chemistry together. Between his code and design and my art and design we produced some memorable moments of visual imagery and gameplay that I am still proud of."

Bob Stevenson

Released
1989

Genre
Platformer

Developer and Publisher
System 3

Stunt Car Racer

"While Geoff Crammond went on to focus on realistic F1 games, nothing can beat the offbeat appeal of Stunt Car Racer. The insane tracks, with all of their loops and jumps, provide an exhilarating rollercoaster ride. While a tad jerky, it's still an amazing technical achievement and so addictive too. The number of times I must have wrecked my car, but I kept coming back for more."

Phil King

Released
1989

Genre
Racing

Developer
Geoff Crammond

Publisher
MicroStyle

Citadel

"Many shoot 'em up games pit you against a relentless and totally predictable onslaught of foes. Citadel was my stab for the 'thinking' player who occasionally wanted to stop and consider what to do next, by making all traps, weapons and gate switches triggered by proximity. By creating futuristic cities on twin levels linked by lift shafts, each choice of move and direction on their tiled floors determined what happened next, thus combining the strategy of a boardgame with elements of an adventure game, plus plenty of blasting action along the way."

Martin Walker

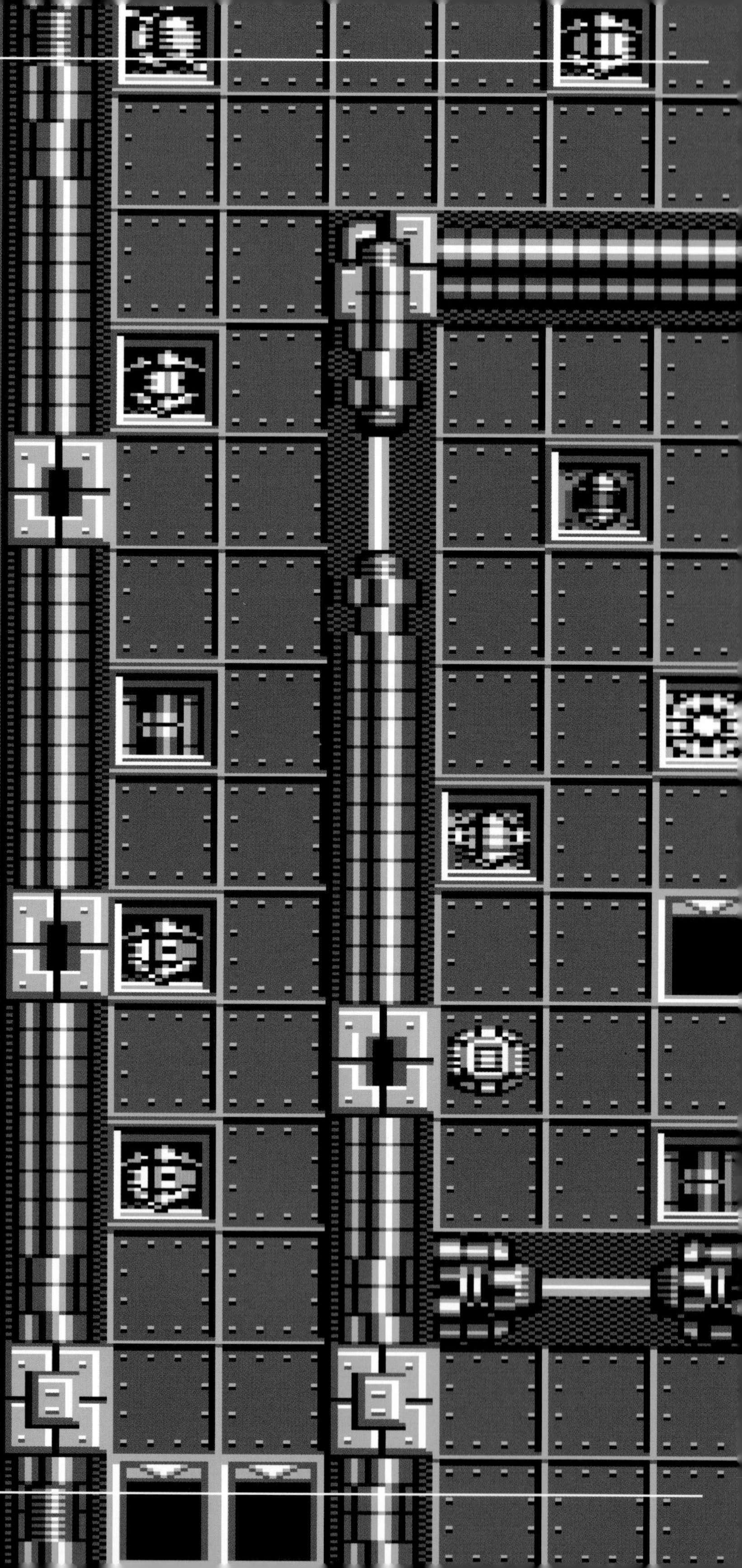

Released
1989

Genre
Puzzle shooter

Developer
Martin Walker

Publisher
Electric Dreams

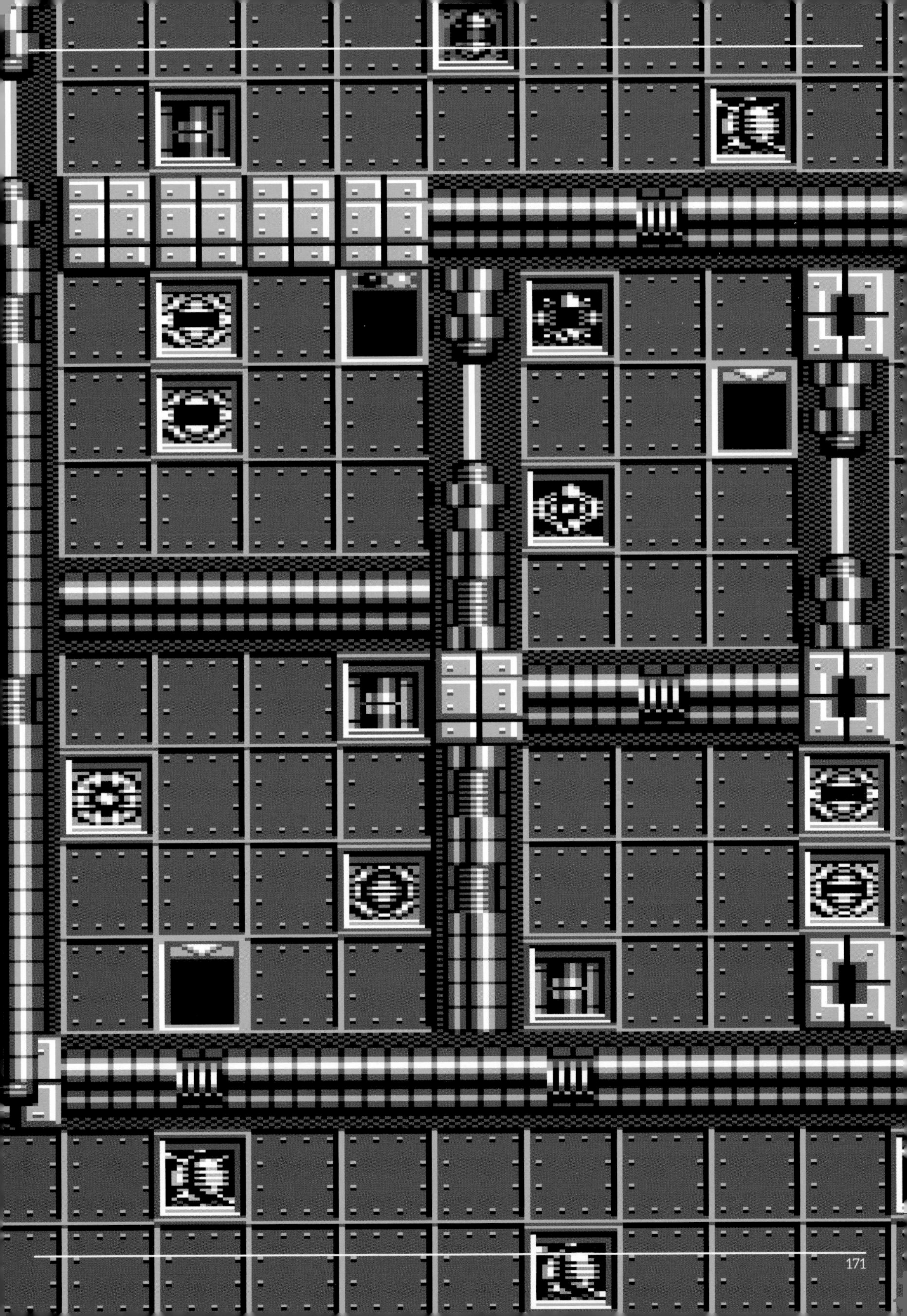

Space Rogue

"It took until 1989 for a worthy successor to Elite to emerge and Space Rogue did just that, taking the strong storyline of an Origin adventure and putting it into the limitless possibilities of space, adding gripping combat to boot. A well deserved Gold Medal in Zzap!64, Space Rogue remains an underappreciated classic."

Robin Hogg

Released
1989

Genre
Simulation

Developer and Publisher
Origin Systems

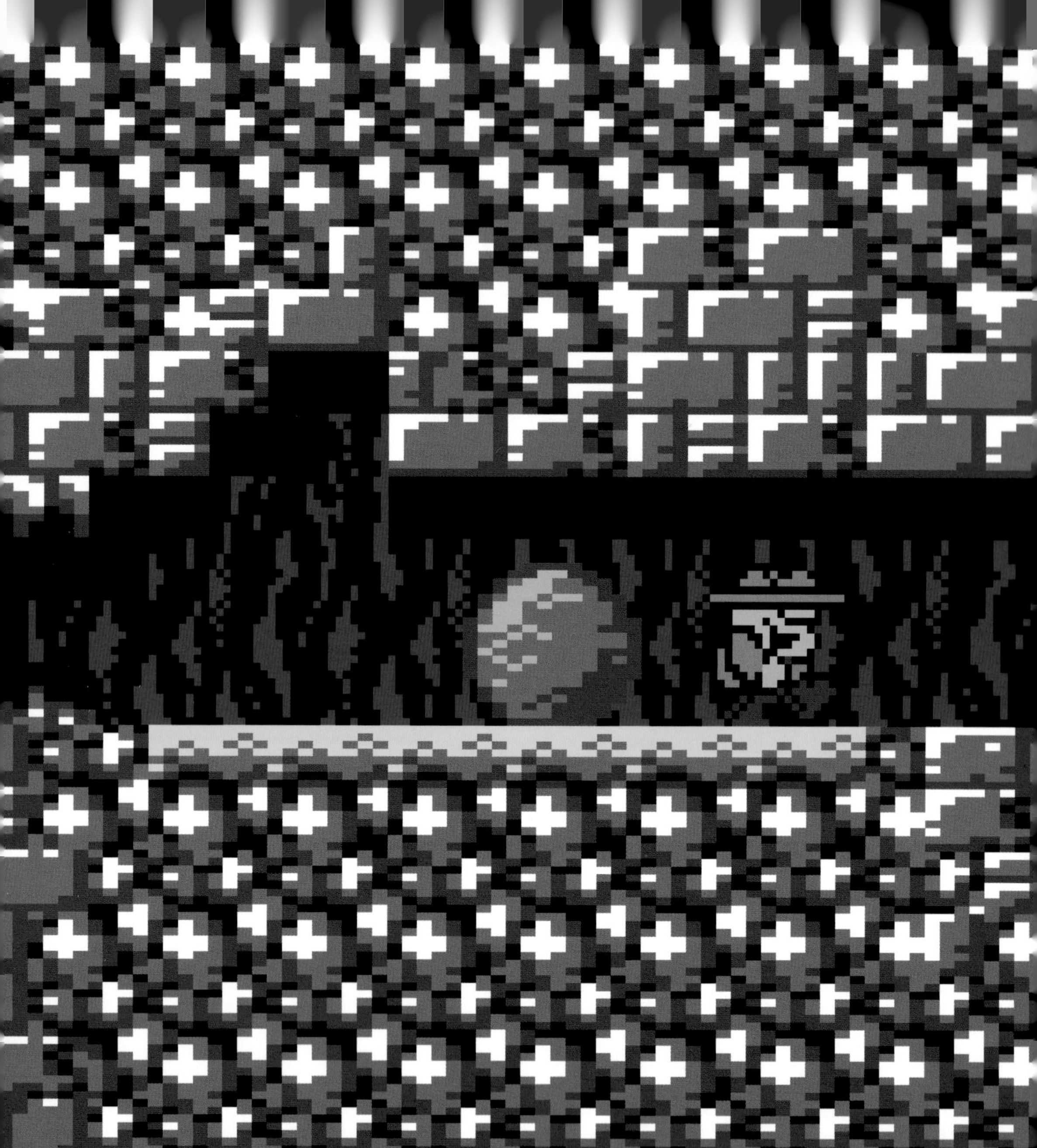

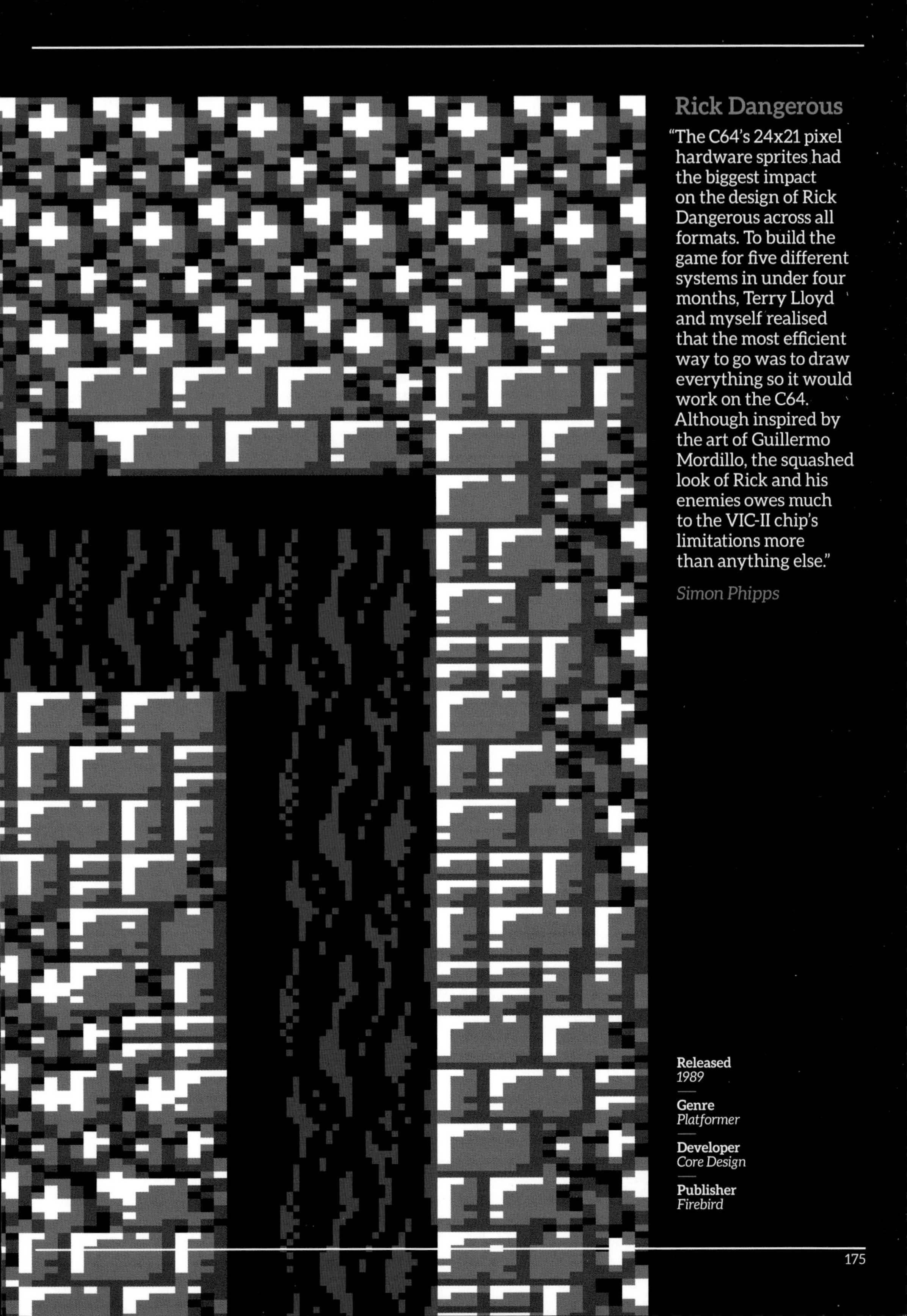

Rick Dangerous

"The C64's 24x21 pixel hardware sprites had the biggest impact on the design of Rick Dangerous across all formats. To build the game for five different systems in under four months, Terry Lloyd and myself realised that the most efficient way to go was to draw everything so it would work on the C64. Although inspired by the art of Guillermo Mordillo, the squashed look of Rick and his enemies owes much to the VIC-II chip's limitations more than anything else."

Simon Phipps

Released
1989

Genre
Platformer

Developer
Core Design

Publisher
Firebird

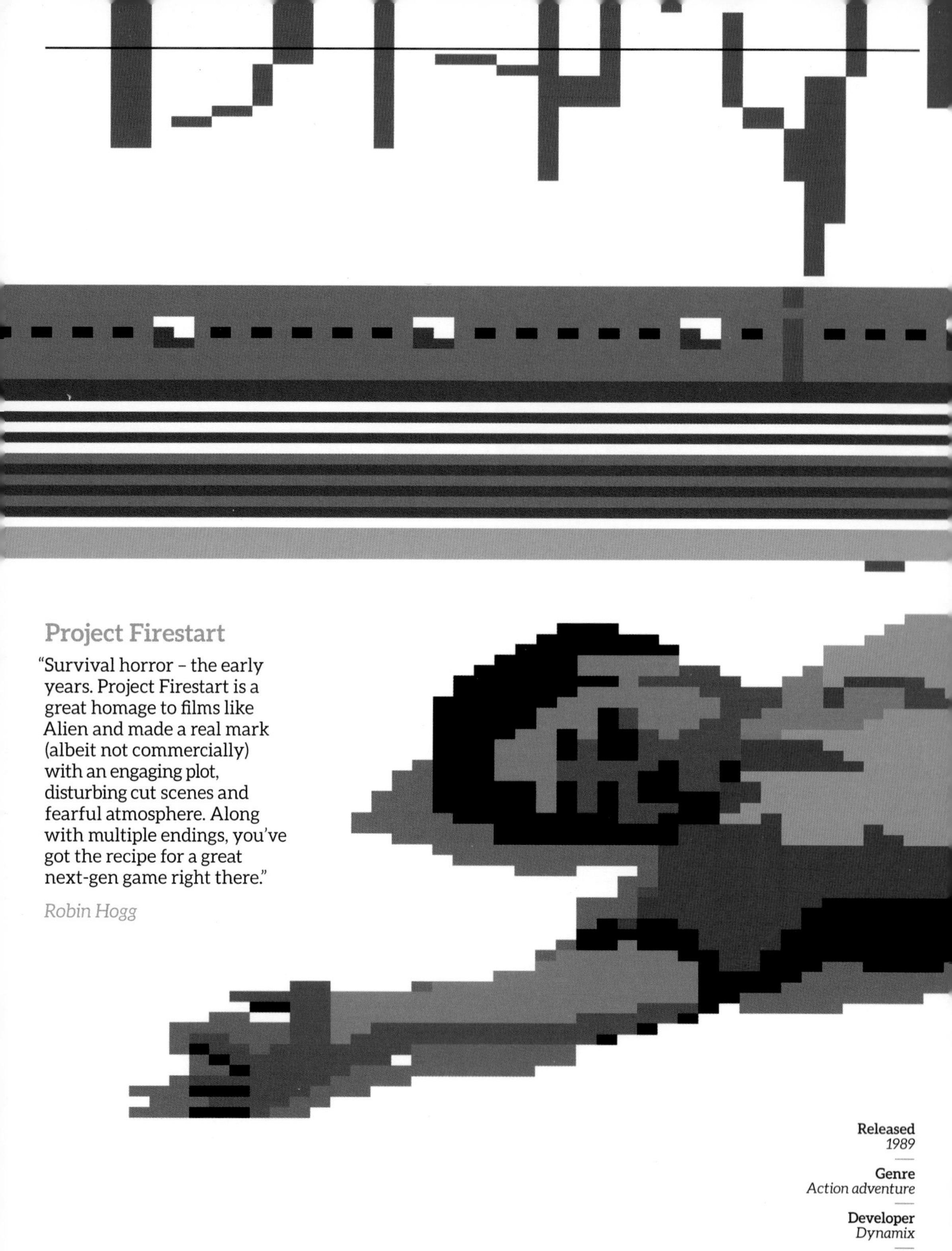

Project Firestart

"Survival horror – the early years. Project Firestart is a great homage to films like Alien and made a real mark (albeit not commercially) with an engaging plot, disturbing cut scenes and fearful atmosphere. Along with multiple endings, you've got the recipe for a great next-gen game right there."

Robin Hogg

Released
1989

Genre
Action adventure

Developer
Dynamix

Publisher
Electronic Arts

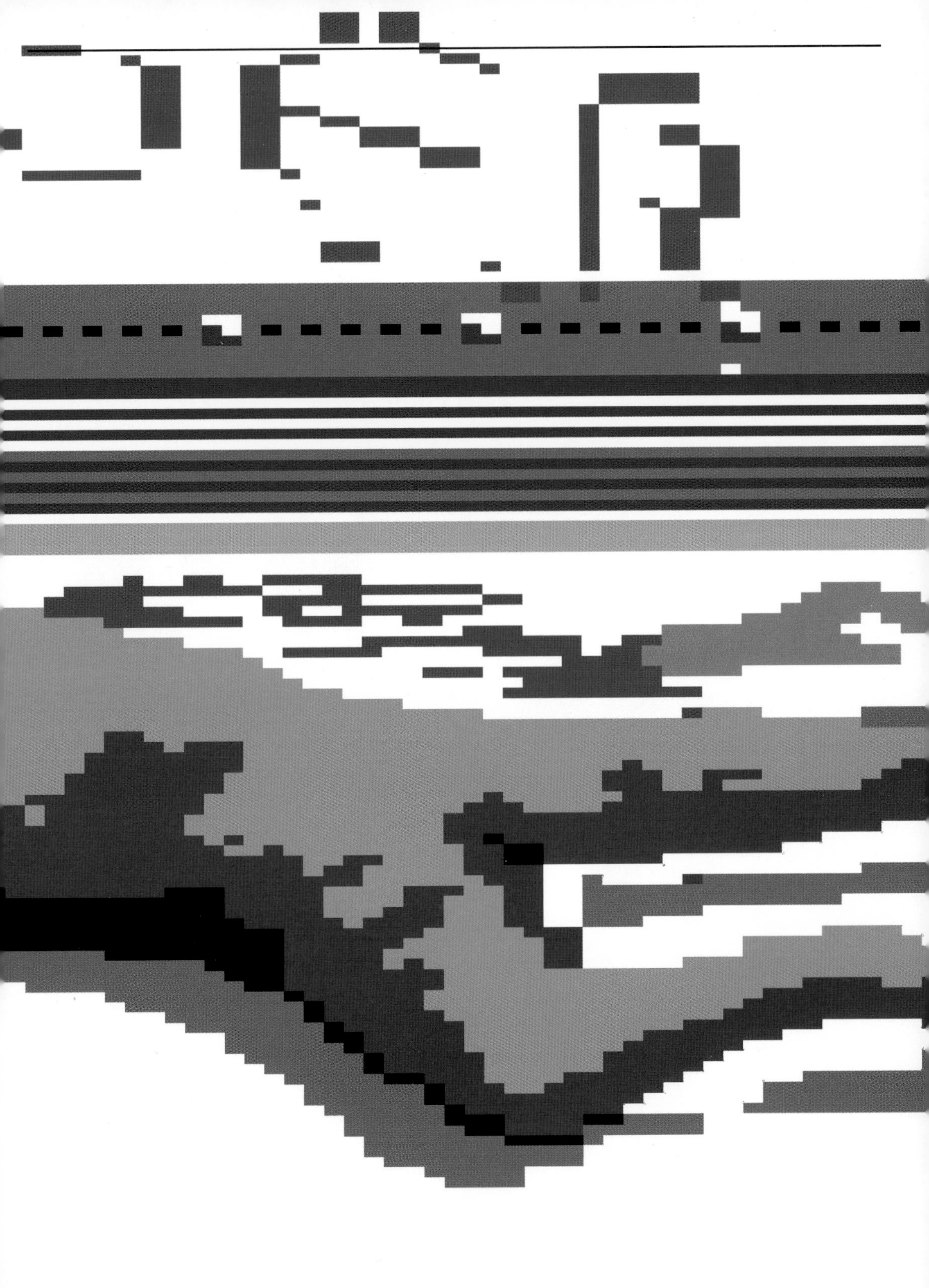

Released *1989* / Genre *Action* / Developer and Publisher *Ocean*

RoboCop

"I remember going to a computer show at Earls Court armed with a newly created RoboCop bitmap. By unbelievable chance, Ocean were looking for an artist for their new RoboCop game. Gary Bracey saw my image and I got the job on the spot! At literally the last minute I had to add some blurb about the video release and until a few months ago I had never noticed the typo. Oh dear!"

Stephen Ian Thomson

Released *1989* / Genre *Action* / Developer and Publisher *Ocean*

The Untouchables

"I had to make a lot of likeness tweaks to actors due to copyright issues. I believe this was the reason Bob Wakelin was commissioned to paint an alternative cover for the game. This was never used, but it looked so cool I had to use it as the title page! Due to the resolution issue on the C64 I did a small section from the centre."

Stephen Ian Thomson

Released *1990* / **Genre** *Platformer* / **Developer and Publisher** *Ocean*

Navy SEALS

"For the title screen I really wanted to do a sort of graphic novel which essentially wou be a flip book of screen I don't think this had been done before. With the game being on a cartridge we were able to fit a lot more on – unfortunately tim was against us and I wa unable to do this. We settled on the logo for the title screen. It came out OK but I hate the lack of anti-aliasing!"

Stephen Ian Thomson

Released *1990* / **Genre** *Rail shooter* / **Developer and Publisher** *Ocean*

Operation Thunderbolt

"This was a 'get it done now' project. I think we had about six week start to end to complet the whole thing. I don't think they even wante a loading screen, but I ended up doing one in my own time while the game was being tested Paul Hughes slipped it in at the last minute. I think I copied this from a movie poster. Can you guess which one?!"

Stephen Ian Thomson

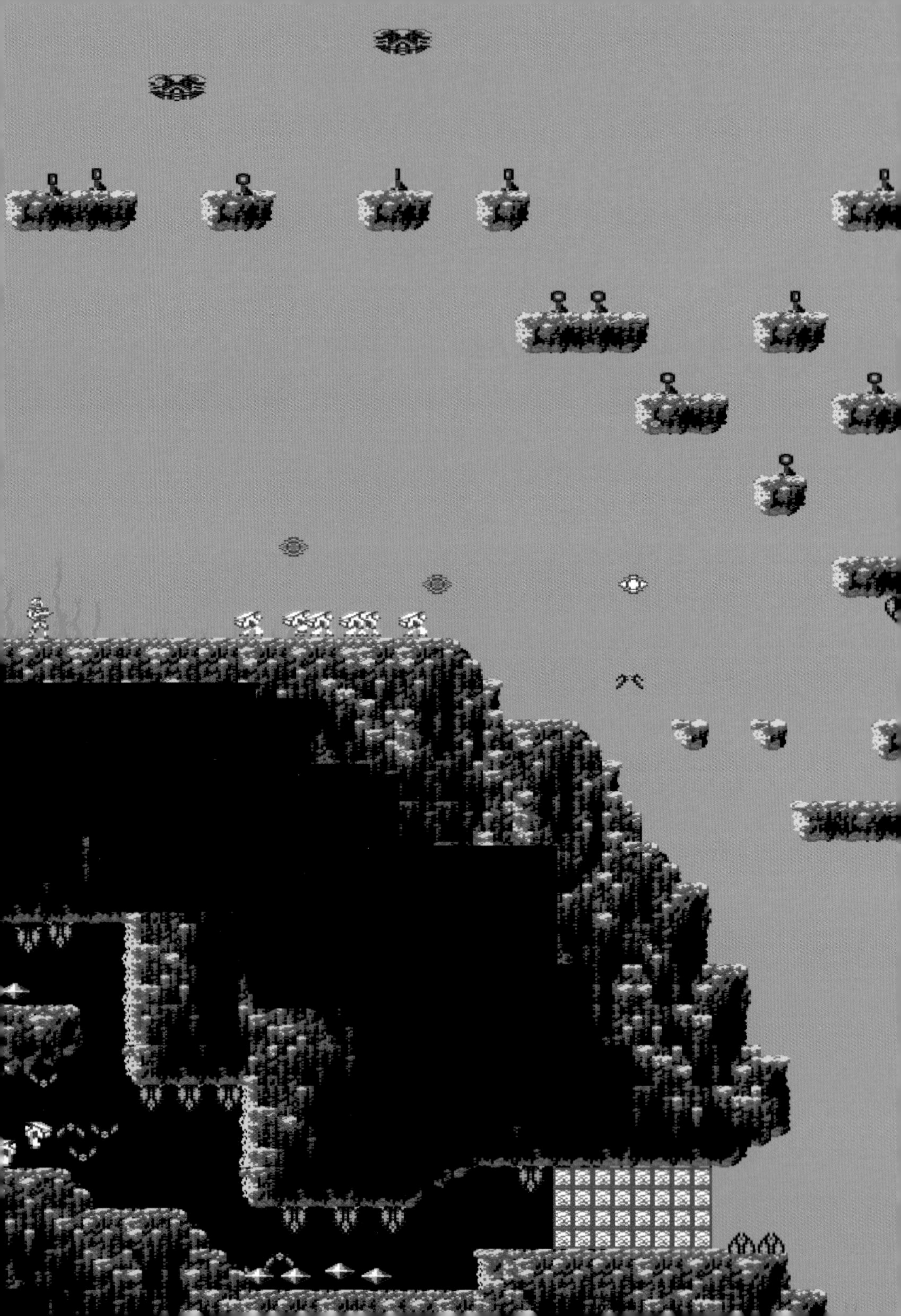

Turrican

"I have a vivid memory of first seeing Turrican in the Zzap!64 office: we were all blown away by it, particularly the graphical variety of the vast labyrinthine levels and some awesome bosses. This is matched by the amazing arsenal of the hero, including the trademark rotating power beam and innovative gyroscope. The gameplay is superbly designed and well balanced."

Phil King

Released
1990

Genre
Platformer

Developer and Publisher
Rainbow Arts

Hammerfist

"I originally created this on the Atari ST and reproduced it by hand on the C64. I was an admirer of the Vivid Image team and Hugh Riley in particular was a graphics hero of mine, so it felt like an honour. The game was gritty and complex but the central idea of swapping characters during play was absolutely at the heart of the game, and what I wanted to convey in the title screen."

Paul Docherty

"This was the first game we made as Vivid Image. The core idea was to ease the pain of dying and then restarting, as when your health was low you could switch to the alternate character while the other recharged. The tough male and the athletic female had different but complimentary skills that needed to be used strategically throughout the game."

Hugh Riley

Released
1990

Genre
Beat 'em up

Developer
Vivid Image

Publisher
Activision

Fantasy World Dizzy

"Development started on the 1st September 1989 and was completed by the end of the month. Fantasy World Dizzy was considered the Oliver's best Dizzy game ever. It was a fun period of our lives... amazingly productive. We'd got loads of money from previous games royalties, we'd bought a house, turned one of the rooms into an office and had no distractions. We'd mastered all the technology and were able to create games very fast and very high quality. The gamers loved them and we were pretty assured that each would go on to sell hundreds of thousands of copies and become best sellers."

Philip Oliver

Released
1990

Genre
Platformer

Developer
The Oliver Twins

Publisher
Codemasters

Creatures

Conceived while we were doing the dishes, Creatures marked a departure from our previous shoot 'em up games and set the tone for the remaining C64 titles we would create. We worked tirelessly on this title, working 18-hour days for the last six weeks of production and going without any sleep over the final five days! We have fond memories of the Thalamus stand at one of the computer shows being literally ripped apart by fans clamouring for the promotional fluffy fuzzy bugs."

John Rowlands

Released
1990

Genre
Puzzle platformer

Developer
Apex Computer Productions

Publisher
Thalamus

Flimbo's Quest

"The Amiga had just come onto the market and we were unsure which machine to initially program Flimbo's Quest on. We had such a good development system on the C64 so we chose that. During development we had a bit of a crisis as Mario moved to Germany and I started to work for a design agency. In the end Laurens did a terrific job in programming Flimbo's Quest and it became a sort of cult game that was successful on both the C64 and Amiga."

Jacco Van 't Riet

Released
1990

Genre
Platformer

Developer and Publisher
System 3

CJ's Elephant Antics

"I was asked to think of a cute character so I came up with an elephant with big floppy ears, and just to throw the cuteness upside down we had him chuck bombs and spit out peanuts. As for the maps and enemies, well I always wanted to draw the Eiffel Tower, the Pyramids and a snowy level with a cute snow monster! The intro was a nod to my all-time favourite Indiana Jones film where CJ bursts out of a plane flying through the air."

Jonathan Smyth Temples

Released
1991

Genre
Platformer

Developer
Genesis Software

Publisher
Codemasters

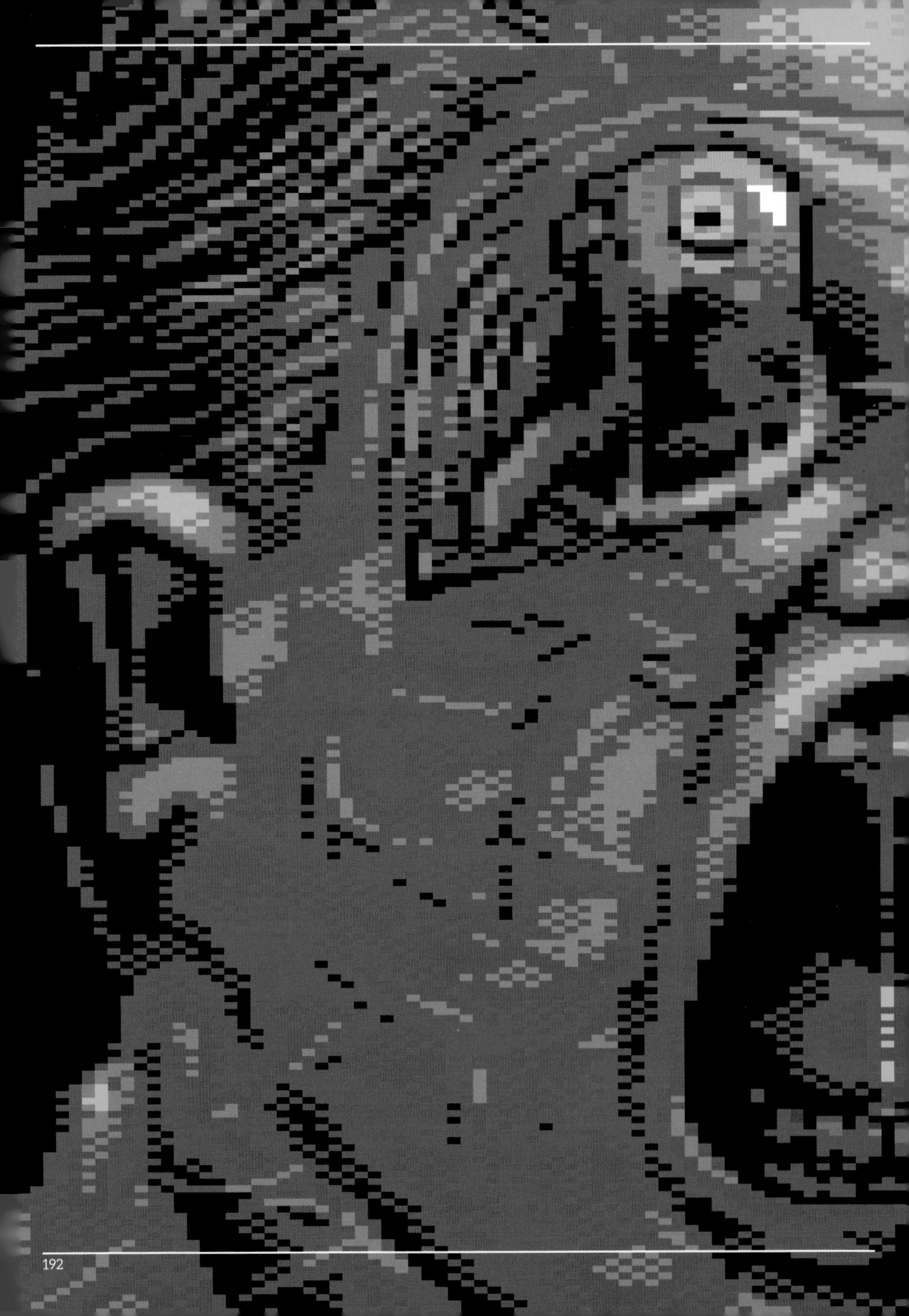

Total Recall

"Total Recall was another 'get it done' project! I had already made a lot of screens for the game, some of which I had to draw from memory. Almost at the very end of the project we got some production stills from the movie, one of which was the eye bulge scene. I had seen the movie by this point, and had to include the Cohaagen death scene. It's one of the funniest things I've ever seen and still makes me laugh to this day."

Stephen Ian Thomson

Released
1991

Genre
Platformer

Developer and Publisher
Ocean

Chase HQ II

Released
1990

Genre
Racing

Developer
Probe Software

Publisher
Ocean

Artwork
Oliver Frey

Turrican II

Released
1991

Genre
Platformer

Developer and Publisher
Rainbow Arts

Artwork
Oliver Frey

Supremacy

"Supremacy (Overlord in the US) was an 8-bit conversion of a 16-bit game with masses of data to display in text and icons. There was no animation so it was an interesting break for me. The tricky part was getting the look and feel of the original while losing none of the functionality. It was very satisfying to get the layout to maximum efficiency and squeeze it all into the C64."

Hugh Riley

Released
1991

Genre
Strategy

Developer
Probe Software

Publisher
Melbourne House

Turbo Charge

"While I'm not a huge fan of the game, I hugely enjoyed producing all of the artwork. It was probably the closest I got to comic work at the time as I had the freedom to create imagery that illustrated one small aspect of a bigger story. In this image we show the player smashing through a border. Not so sure about the depiction of the car, but I really like what I did with the three cops, especially the poor fellow rolling over the hood!"

Robin Levy

Released
1991

Genre
Racing

Developer and Publisher
System 3

Exile

"This was the last loading screen I created for the C64. I was a huge fan of Jeremy Smith's Thrust, so there was no chance I was going to turn the opportunity down! For the astronaut I wanted to evoke a shiny helmeted face, and the brown blobs on the helmet are supposed to be reflections of approaching aliens. It was tough to return to the C64's limitations after working for a year on 16-bit platforms."

Paul Docherty

Released
1991

Genre
Action adventure

Developer and Publisher
Audiogenic

Last Ninja 3

"Last Ninja 3 was an event for me when it finally came out and was available in stores. The controls and gameplay were quirky, but the series and games as a whole are the absolute example of artistic achievement from the C64. There was not a part of these games that wasn't the best the medium could offer – the art, the music, even down to the covers of the games themselves. A design triumph that stands tall amongst games of today and likely forever."

Marc Bell

Released
1991

Genre
Action adventure

Developer and Publisher
System 3

SMASH
TV
99

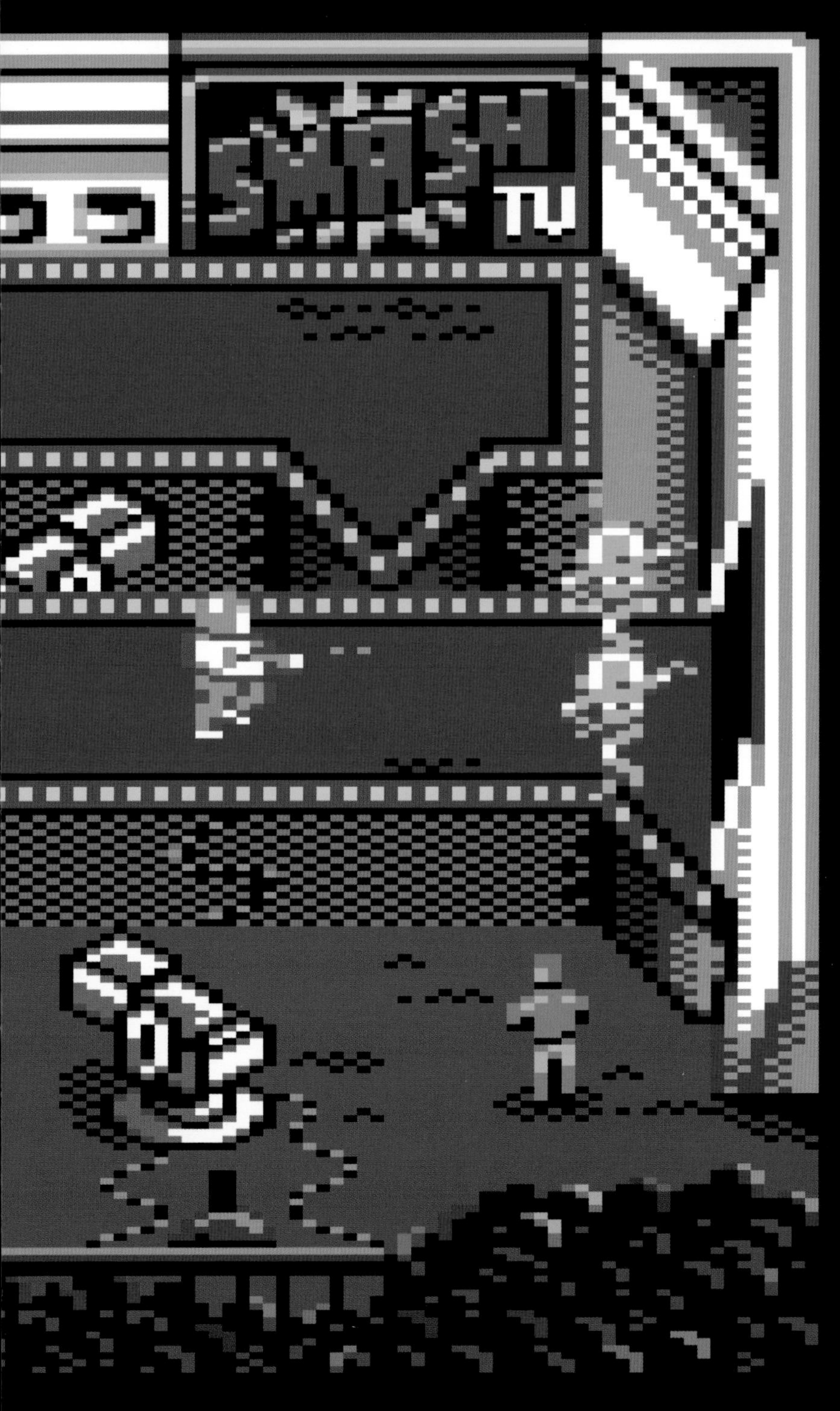

Smash TV

"The original Smash TV arcade machine (made in 1990) by veteran game designer Eugene Jarvis at Williams, tried to predict what TV would be like far off in the future of 1999. It had a fun game design mechanic which (amusingly) became the core DNA of many reality TV shows today. (You'd work as a team in multiplayer mode, but when the prizes show up, it's an absolute grab-fest!) Watch out for Mutoid man!"

Dave Perry

Released
1991

Genre
Run and gun

Developer
Probe Software

Publisher
Ocean

Slicks

"In 1992 Codemasters developed a great top-down F1 racing game for the C64. Slicks features six tracks, multiplayer, six unique F1 cars, smooth scrolling, ruthless AI and a Career mode which persisted with your team for the next season. Just like real F1 you have to try to get a ride in your opponents' superior F1 teams like Brabham and McLaren. It's easy to see why Codemasters are still creating amazing racing games today."

Andy Hayes

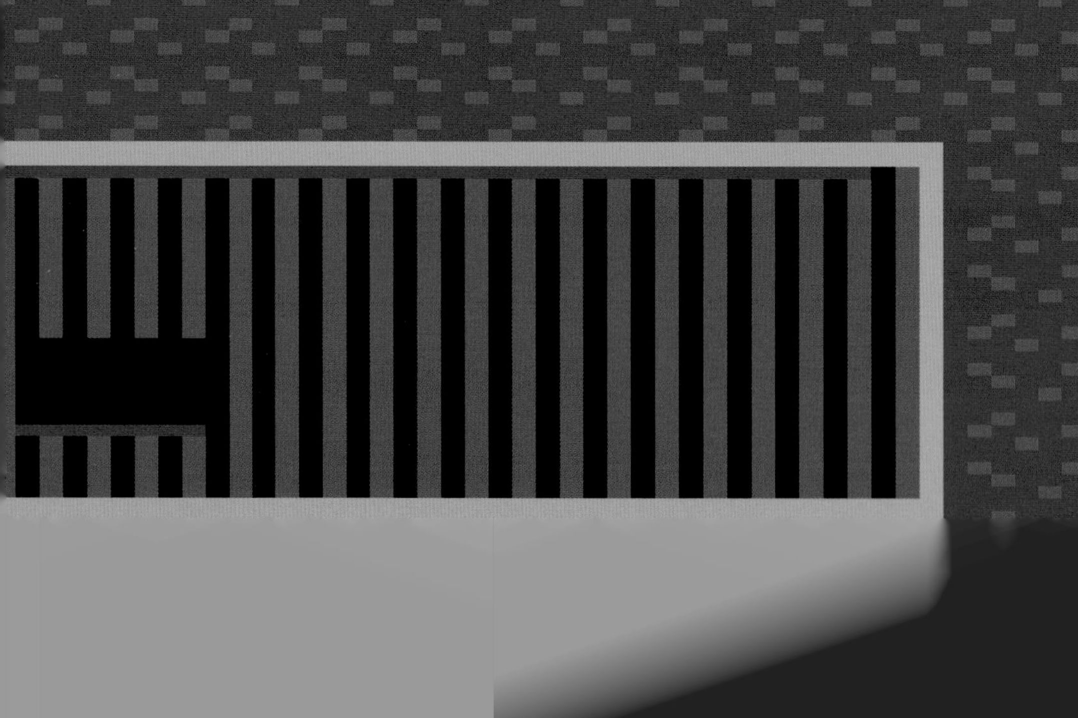

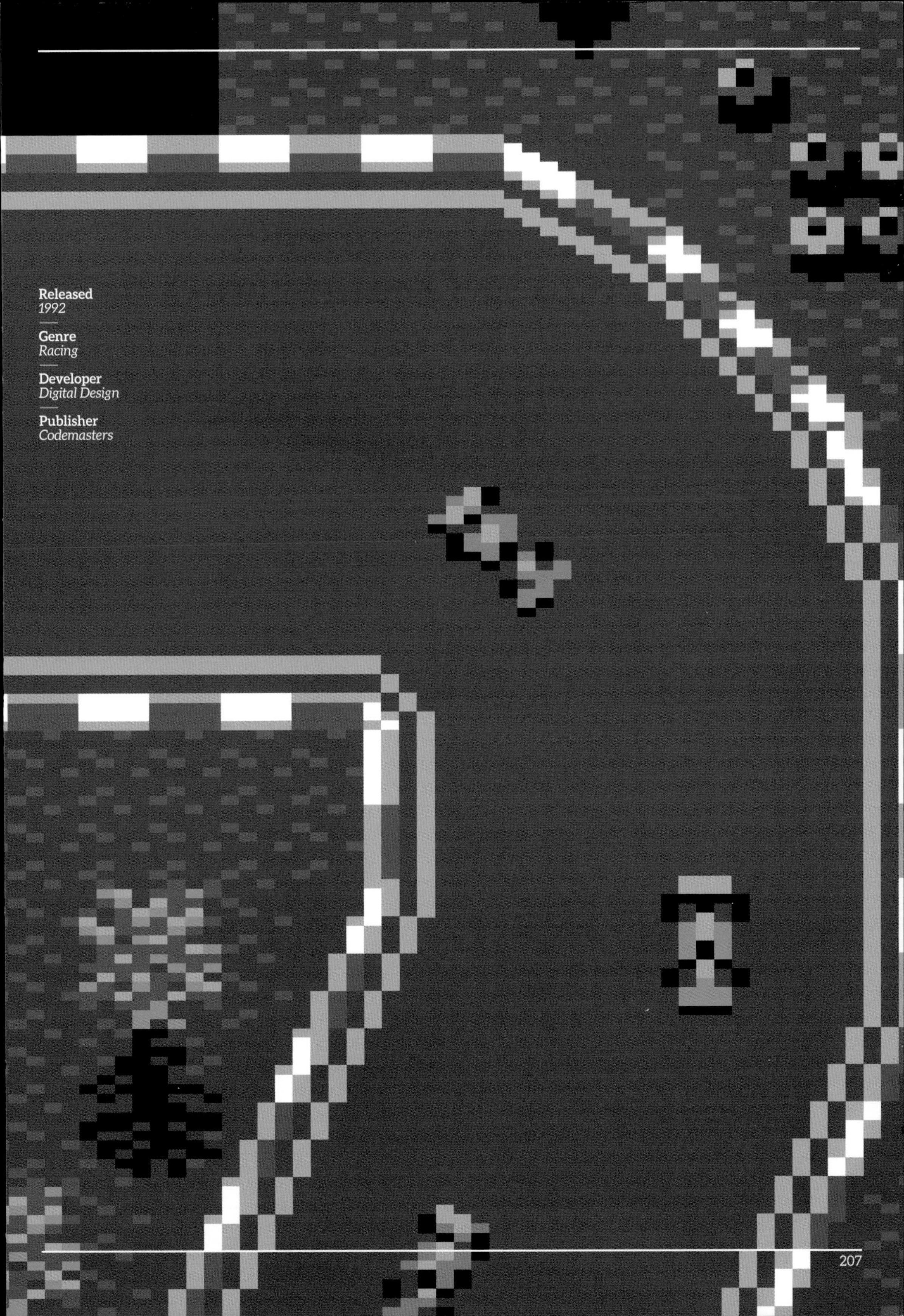

Released
1992

Genre
Racing

Developer
Digital Design

Publisher
Codemasters

> "We helped with the initial bunch of games that were put on the C64GS system. It was a great idea but unfortunately, Commodore couldn't quite pull it off."

Mevlut Dinc, Vivid Image

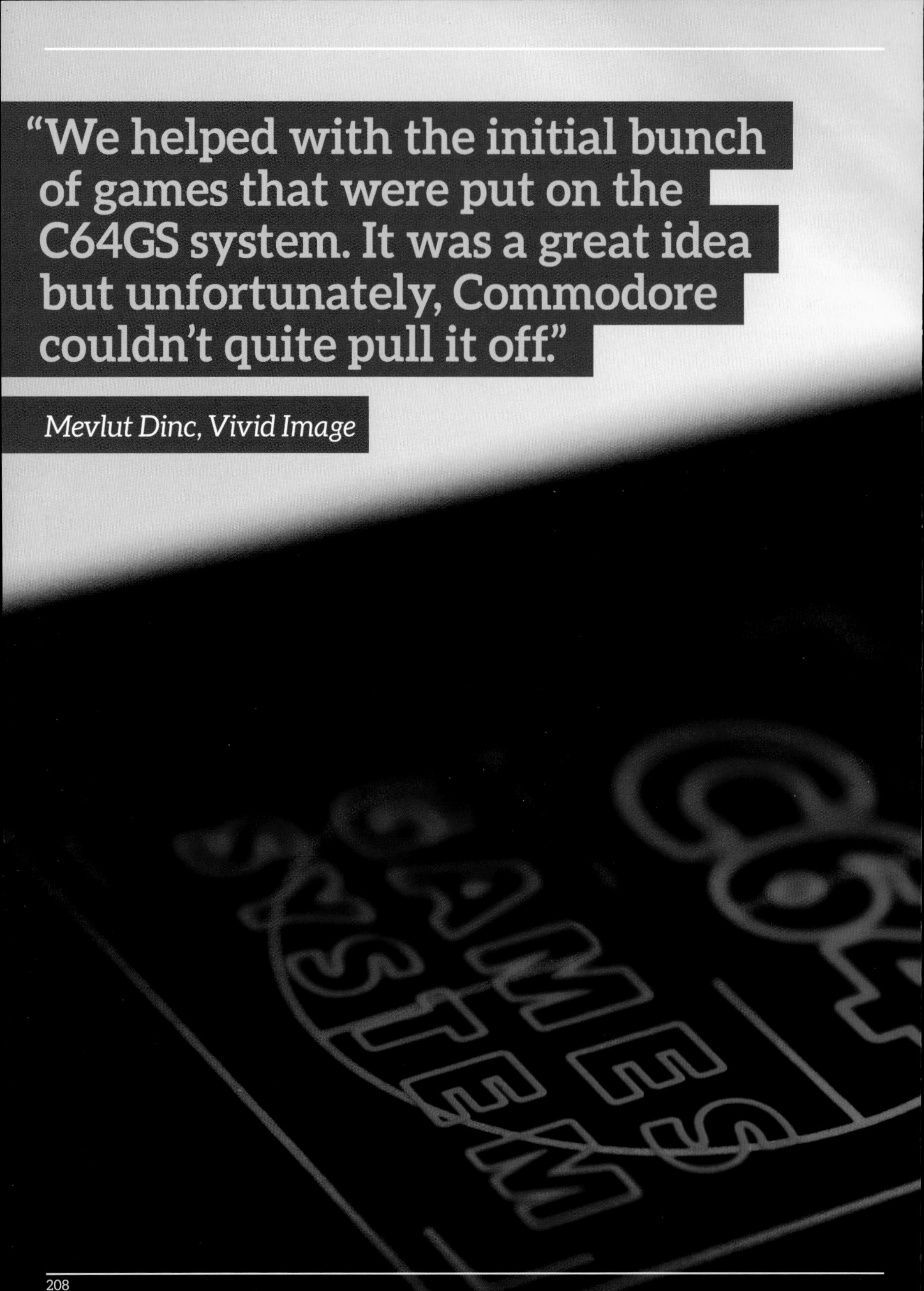

Released
1992

Genre
Platformer

Developer
Vivid Image

Publisher
Image Works

First Samurai

"First Samurai is one of the most remembered and respected games ever, and was voted the game of the year in 1991. It involved so many great programmers and graphics artists. The Amiga was the lead version and we did a great job of fully capturing the game on the C64. We were very lucky to have Jon Williams to code and Mat Sneap to do the graphics for the C64 version."

Mevlut Dinc

Mayhem in Monsterland

"We poured so much love and attention into every aspect of its design that this is the game we're most proud of. We pushed the VIC chip to its limit with the user interface, gameplay and graphics. And although awarded 100% by Commodore Format, which caused many to discuss whether any game could indeed be perfect, it was the perfect swansong for us."

John Rowlands

Released
1993

Genre
Platformer

Developer and Publisher
Apex Computer Productions

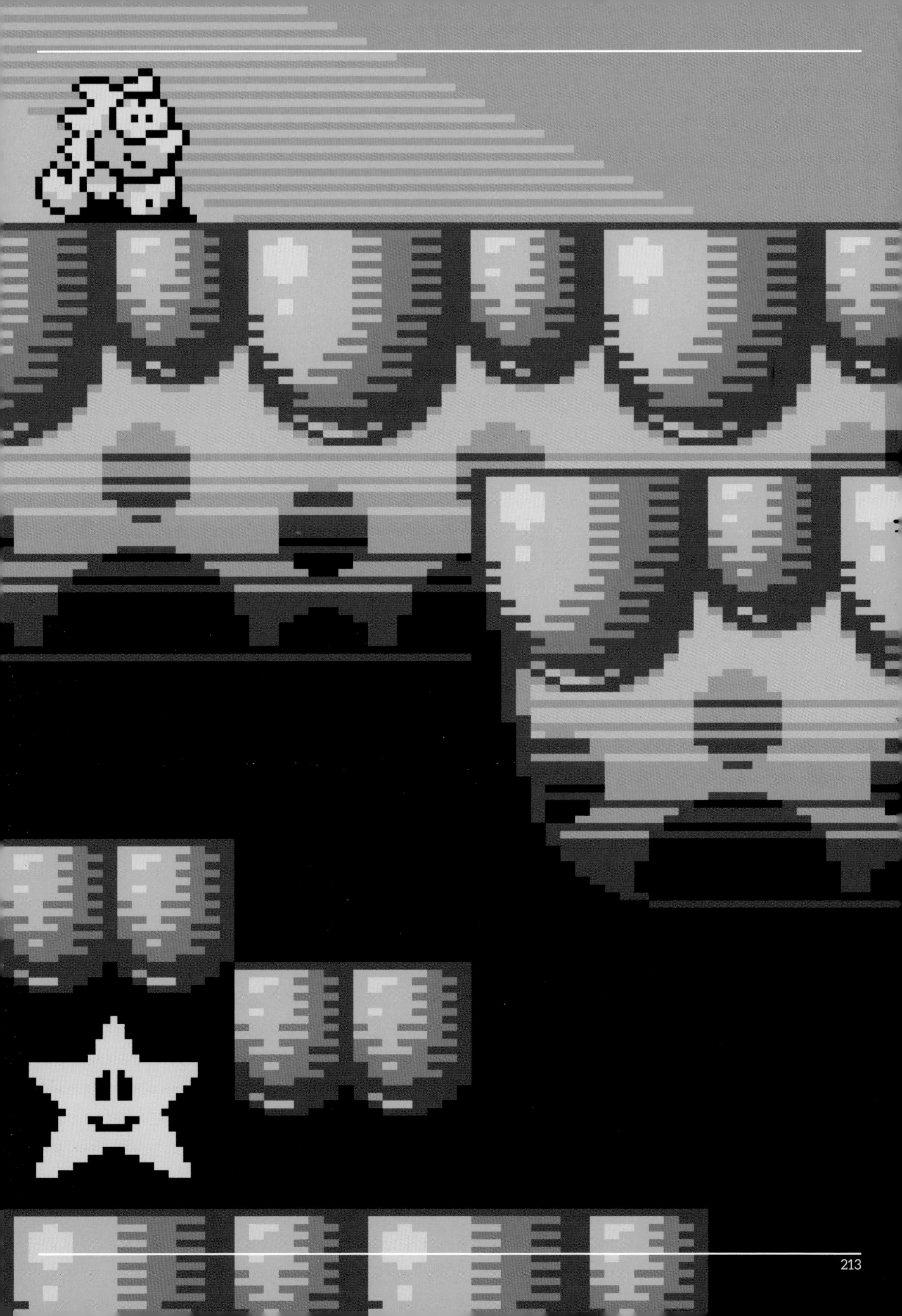

Released
1994

Genre
Puzzle

Developer
E & E Software

Publisher
Psygnosis

Lemmings

"The trapdoor opens and here they come! Argh! Gotta be fast! There's loads of them. Yes, Lemmings is a race against the clock. How do they pack such jaunty personality into a handful of pixels? It's a work of geniu… no! I need a blocker! They're heading towards the lava! It's hard to write a review whilst trying to save them all. And believe me, I do want to save them all – Lemmings does that to you."

James Leach

Prince of Persia

"Several people were talking about the viability of a C64 version at the time and my intention was to create some game assets for possible public domain use. Coincidently, a programmer named Andreas Varga had also been creating Prince for the C64 on cartridge but he lacked finished graphics. By that happy coincidence the C64 finally got Prince of Persia, albeit 20 years late! I was very happy with the 'Sizzler' rating in Retro Gamer magazine and original creator Jordan Mechner praising it on the development blog."

Steven Day

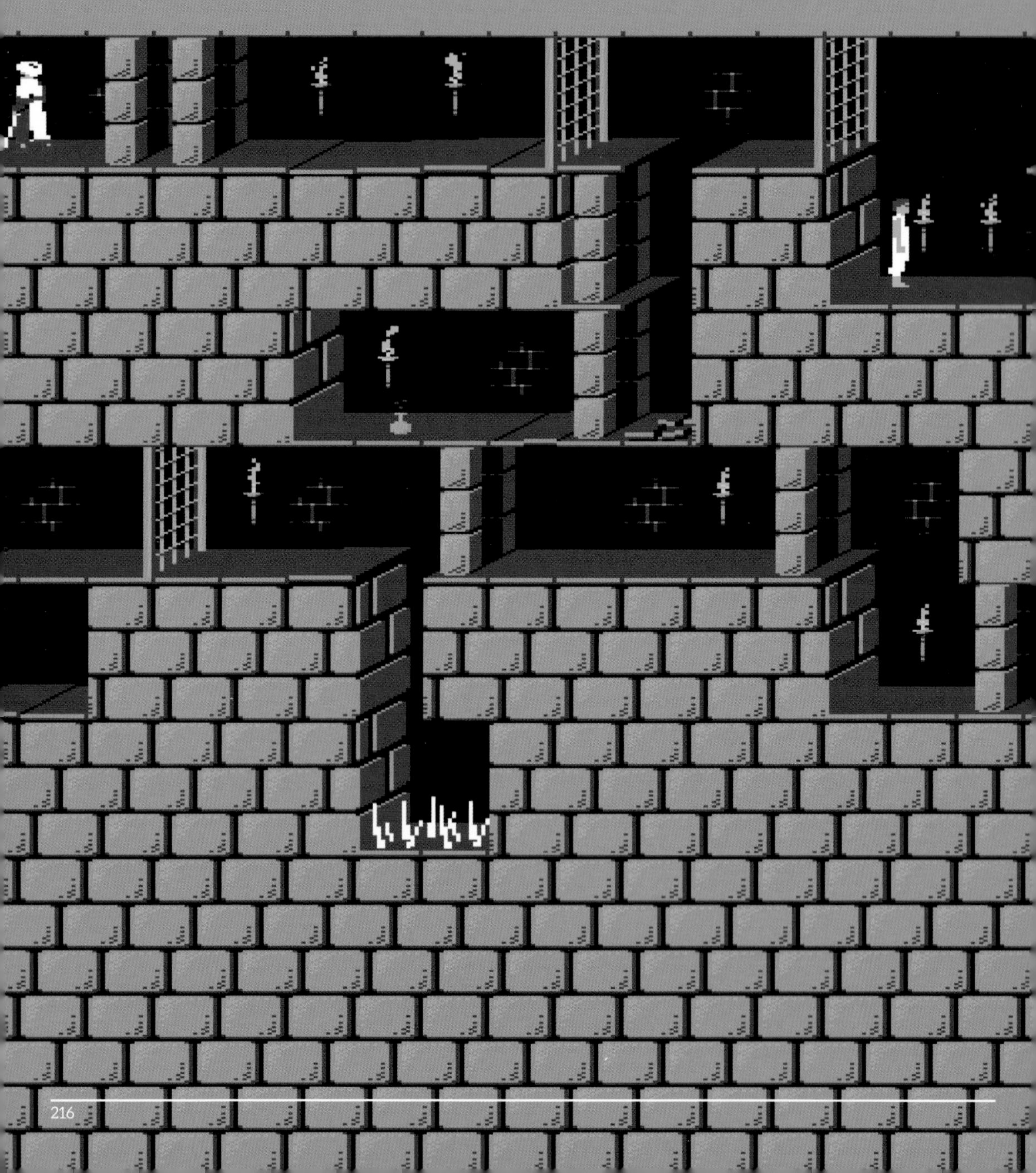

Released
2011

Genre
Platformer

Developer
Andreas Varga

Publisher
Public Domain

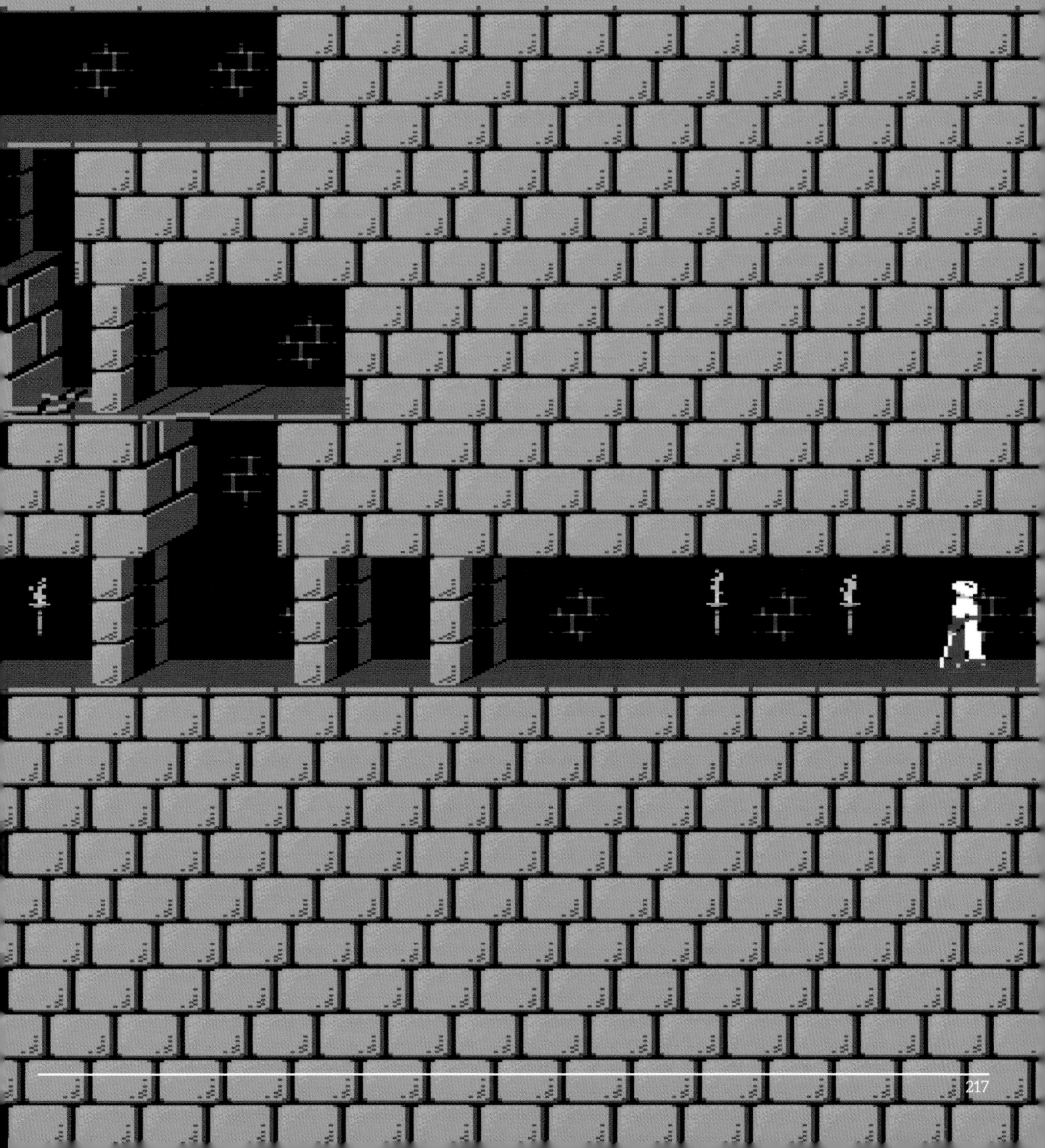

C64anabalt

"After playing the Flash version of Canabalt in 2009, I knew it would be fun to try to convert to the C64. The gameplay, as well as the grey colour scheme, was something that would work well on the breadbox. Most importantly, the scale of the game was small enough for me not to lose motivation halfway through. Unfortunately, some things from the original that I wanted to include did not make it to the final game due to memory limitations."

Paul Koller

Released
2011

Genre
Endless runner

Developer
Paul Koller

Publisher
RGCD

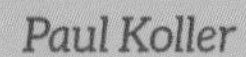

Super Bread Box

"The 2010 game Super Crate Box is often described by Vlambeer themselves as a game that could have existed in the '80s. Well, I proved to them that indeed their concept is very well possible on an 8-bit machine. Besides the obvious multiplexor and weapon effects, the playable characters were also a challenge to implement. It was not easy to convert the characters to only six double-sized pixels across, but in the end I think I succeeded nicely!"

Paul Koller

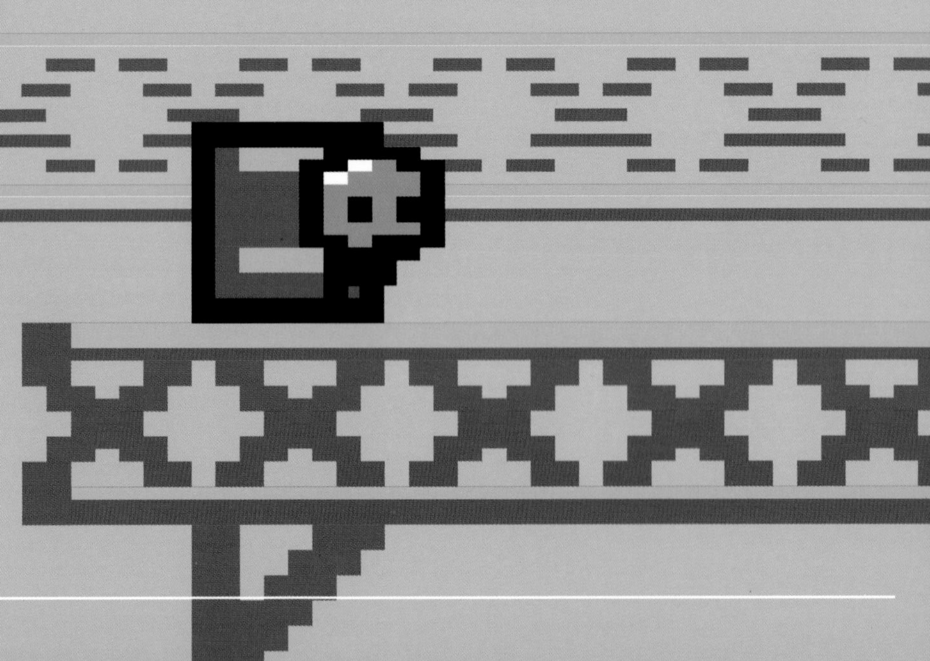

Released
2013

Genre
Action

Developer
Paul Koller

Publisher
RGCD

Bomberland

"This game is quite a considerable part of my life. The time between the first line of code typed and the last was longer than the entire official life of the Commodore 64! It was worth it though and the library of games on the C64 has been enriched with a fully-fledged entry of the Bomberman series."

Michal Okowicki

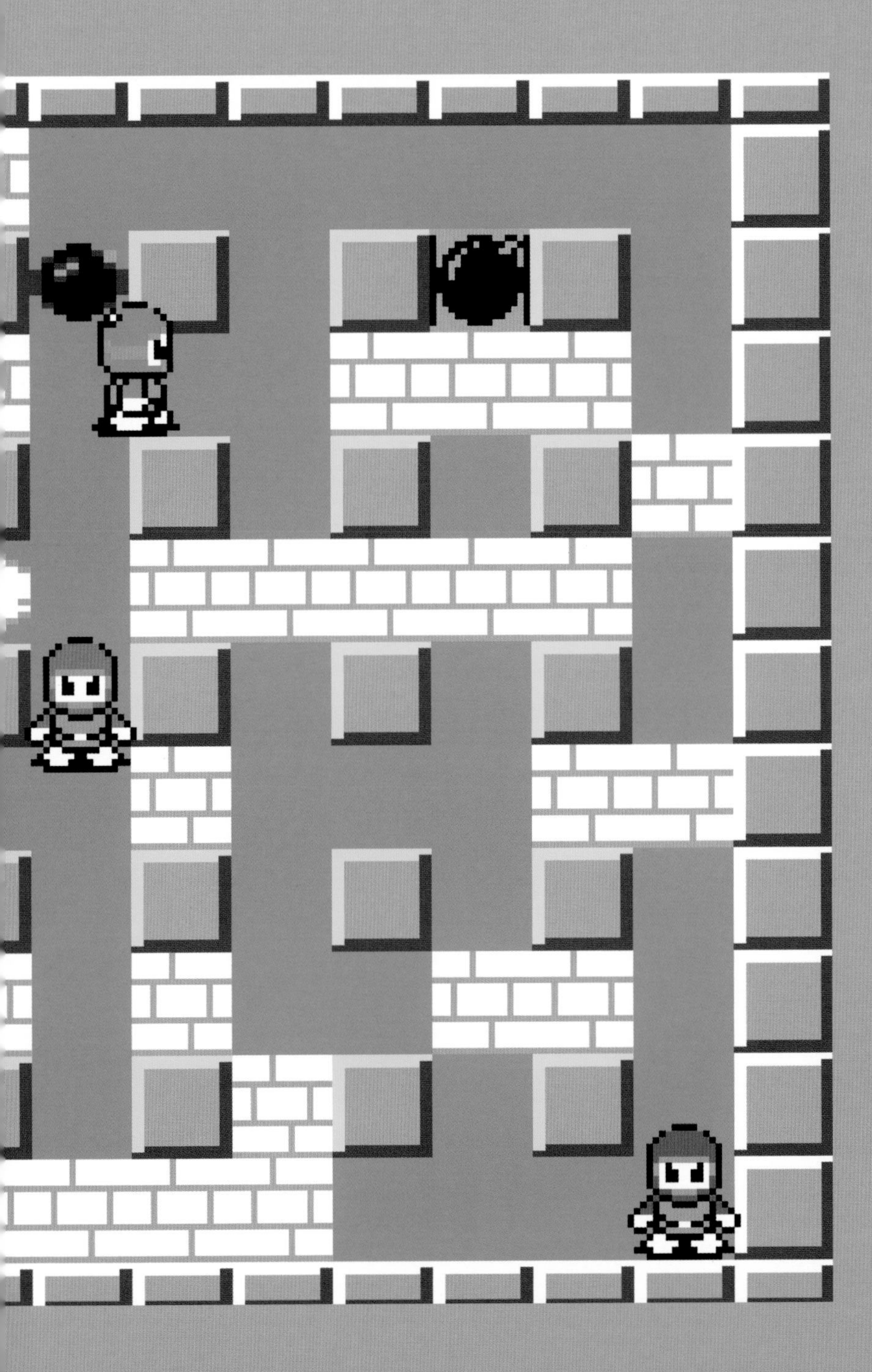

Released
2013

Genre
Action

Developer
Michal Okowicki

Publisher
RGCD

Micro Hexagon

"I always wanted to try my hand at a vector-type game, but without the slow movement usually associated with such games on the C64. Super Hexagon is a fantastic twitch-style arcade game that intrigued me to see whether I could pull something off like this. After releasing the game in December 2013 I was overwhelmed by the attention this port received!"

Paul Koller

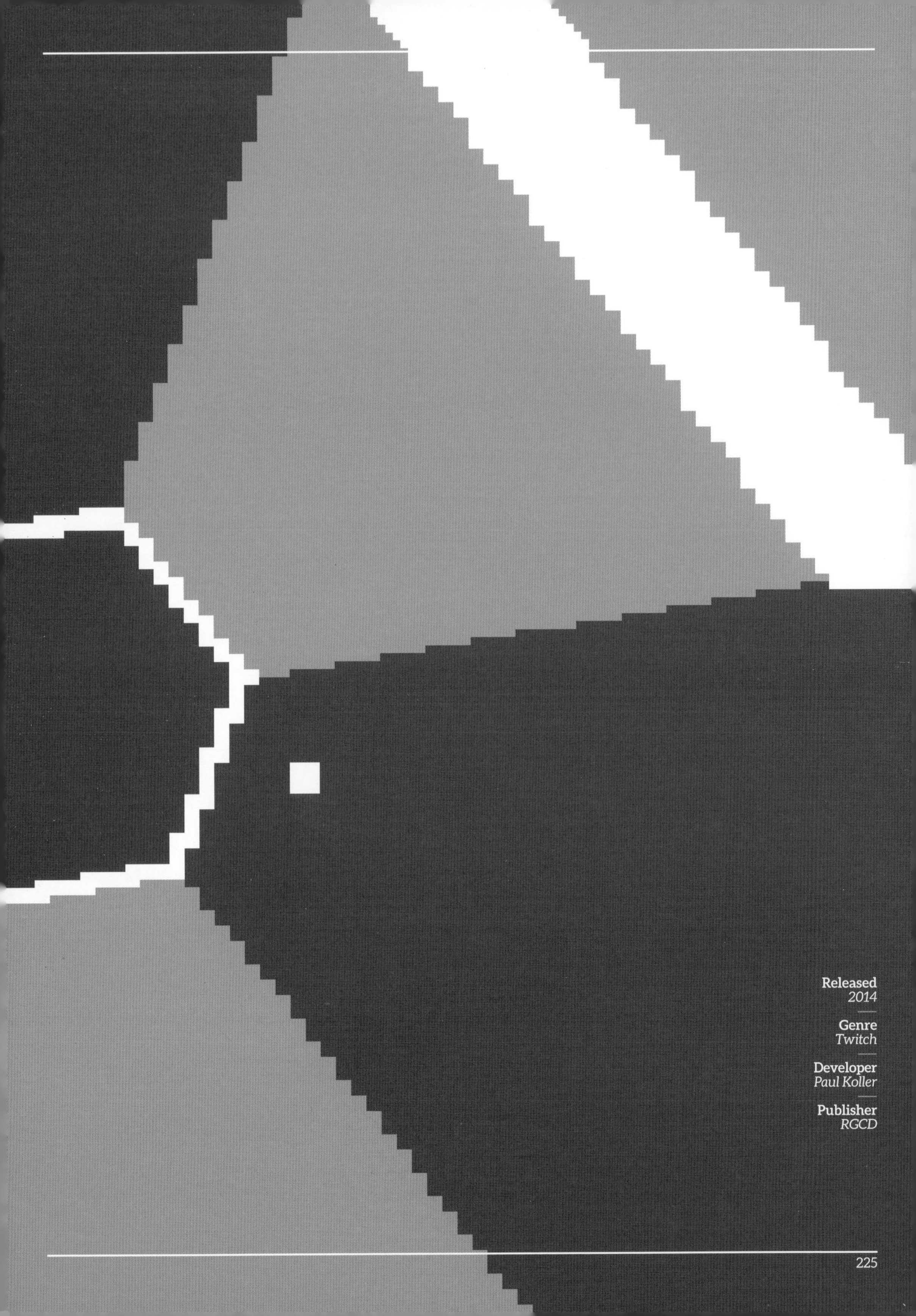

Released
2014

Genre
Twitch

Developer
Paul Koller

Publisher
RGCD

Commando

"I endeavoured to produce a screen with the feel of a much expanded version. The main image had exactly what I needed: a 'Band of Brothers' worn-looking soldier with a netted helmet and festooned with grenades and ammo clips (just like the game). Around him I added as many of the familiar game elements as I could, with special attention to the palm trees and the newly added helicopter, which are what most people remember from the arcade game."

Steven Day

Released
2014

Genre
Run and gun

Developer
Nostalgia

Publisher
Public Domain

A huge thanks to all backers of the Kickstarter campaign!

Aaron Green
Aaron Mahler
Aaron Schnuth
Aaron Smith
Achim Demelt
Achim Kaspers
Adam Dufty
Adam Finzel
Adam Flynn
Adam Jansch
Adam Simpson
Adelaide Andrews
Adrian Brown
Adrian Powici
Ady Simmonds
Alain Bougeniere
Alan Bolger
Al Busby
Alejandro S. Cubel
Alessandro Dorigatti
Alessandro Gambetti
Alessandro Motisi
Alexander Bahr
Alexander Barg
Alexander Klock
Alexander Lincoln
Alexander Walnum
Alexander Young
Alexandra Albrecht
Alex Bunch
Allan Hudgins
Ally Hogg
Amar Sabeta
Anderson Kong
Andrea Beretta
Andrea Maderna
Andreas Altenheimer
Andreas Deublein
Andreas Glaser
Andreas Krebs
Andreas Schnupf
Andreas Varga
Andreas Wanda
Andrea Venturi
Andre Haensel
Andrew Burch
Andrew Crawshaw
Andrew Dean
Andrew Fenner
Andrew Fisher
Andrew Hayes
Andrew Newman
Andrew Ogier
Andrew Simpson
Andrew Stephen
Andrew Stewart
Andy Godoy
Andy Roberts
Andy Taylor
Anne Jan Brouwer
Anne Obriot
Ant Harper
Anthony Ogden
Anthony Stiller
Antoine Griffon
Antonio Furno
Anton MacArthur
Arkadiusz Kaminski
Arnd Beenen
Arto Chydenius
Arvid Weber
Ashley Hogg
Ashley Wakeman
Atle Moen
Attila Fagyal
Ausretrogamer
Axel Gerhardt
Barry Barber
Barry Irvine
Barry Riddiford
Bastian Schoppet
Benjamin Chee
Benjamin Flynn
Benjamin Herzog
Benjamin Wimmer
Ben Scarboro
Ben Wheare
Bidaux Thomas
Bieno M. Braitmaier
Bill Loguidice
Björn Andersson
Björn Endre
Björn Ritzl
Björn Schulz
Blair MacIntyre
BoB Morgan
Bogdan Necula
Bo Gøran Kvamme
Braden Manning
Brad O'Hearne
Brandon Staggs
Brendan Devenney
Brendan Humphreys
Brian Campbell
Brian K. Perry
Briatte Fabien
Bruce Canu
Bruno Del Frate
Bryan Pope
Bryson Whiteman
Byron Jenssen
Cabel Sasser
Caine Jenkins
Calogero Domianello
Cameron Davis
Cameron Wallis
Carlo Luciano Bianco
Carlo Savorelli
Carl Smythe
Carsten Sandtner
Cass Holgate
Cato Færøy
Cécile Antoine Martin
Charles Miller
Chris Abbott
Chris Baker
Chris Doig
Chris Foulds
Chris Hill
Chris Hogan
Chris Howard
Chris Patten
Chris Peel
Chris Schofield
Chris Shrigley
Chris Smith
Chris Stoten
Christian D. Storgaard
Christian Peters
Christian Schaefer
Christian A. Schiller
Christian Woltz
Christoph Bessel
Christopher Hamze
Christopher Just
Christopher Salomon
Christoph Hofmann
Christos Savvides
Chris Van Graas
Chris Wilkins
Chris Wilson
Claudio Bottaccini
Claudio Todeschini
Colin Fulcher
Constantin Gillies
Corinna Vigier
Costantino Gallo
Craig Derbyshire
Craig Dolan
Craig Flaherty
Craig Smuda
Damian Butt
Dana Freeman
Daniela Gebhardt
Daniel Auger
Daniel Brunner
Daniel Dillard
Daniel Dönigus
Daniele Balestrieri
Daniele Gaeta
Daniel Gustafsson
Daniel Illgen
Daniel Johnson
Daniel Mueller
Daniel Peyer
Daniel Renner
Daniel Rethmeier
Daniel Riek
Daniel Skantz
Dani Moya Teruel
Dan Martland
Danny O Welch
Dan Phillips
Dario Duranti
Darren Christie
Darren Jones
Darren Kerr
Darren Osadchuk
Darren Redgrave
Darren Skelton
Dave Cheney
Dave Haylett
Dave Roscoe
Dave Ross
Dave Test
David Bagel
David Belson
David Bulwer
David Cameron
David Celozzi
David Coyles
David Crookes
David C Thompson
David Di Troia
David Gaunt
David Greelish
David Gustafsson
David Kelsall
David Lenaerts
David Lyons
David Martin
David Moreau
David Normington
David Öhlén
David Perry
David Petyt
David Richier
David Sanger
David Saunders
David Simons
David Steiger
David Stenton
David Winter
David Youd
Dean Tobin
Del Cardoso
Derek Birt
Desktop Daydreams
Didier Coll
Diego Barros
Dietmar Hilbrich
Dietmar Schinnerl
Dimitris Gourlis
DonChaos
Don Stanco
Doug Kurcewicz
Dustin Mierau
Dustin Vogel
Edmund Dunbar
Edward Culbreath
Edward Elias
Edward George
Edward Lowry
Edward Taub
Edward Wainwright
Emanuel Brenke
Emanuele Iannone
Erasmus Kuhlmann
Erdem Sen
Eric Nelson
Erik Pede
Ernesto Borio
Ernst Edl
Erwin Andreasen
Eugenio Angueira
Evan Paterson
Fabio De Luca
Fabrizio Pedrazzini
Faizel Mahomed
Fantini Simone
Fazekas Gergely
Ferruccio Cinquemani
F. Gutherz
Filipe Carvalho
Filippo Scaboro
Finn Renard
Flavio N. de Figueiredo
Flemming Dupont
Florent Poiraud
Francesco Brolli
Francesco Pessolano
Franck Martin
François Picot
Frank Arlt
Frank Buss
Frank Cifaldi
Frank Gasking
Franklin Webber
Frank Price
Frank Reitberger
Frederick Ostrander
Fzool
GamesYouLoved
Gareth Darby
Gareth Halfacree
Gareth Owen
Gareth Taft
Gary Dunne
Gary Foreman
Gavin Greenhalgh
Geir Straume
Geoff Wells
Geslin
Giacomo Generali
Giampaolo Frello
Giordano Contestabile
Glen McNamee
Gordon Burke
Gotthard Weiss
Graeme Norval

Graham Sharp
Graham Turner
Graham W Wöbcke
Greg Beck
Gregg Ivers
Gregory Gollinger
Gregory Hammond
Gregory Saunders
G. Sollich
Günter Wallner
Hans-Martin Frey
Hardmeyer Christian
Hasan Ates
Haydn Dalton
Heath Kerwin
Heidi Välkkilä
Heiko Spallek
Hendrik Lesser
Henrik Lindhe
Henri Vilminko
H. Naarlien-Tolpinrud
Holger Meller
Hope Marie Washburne
Hory Fabien
Howard Knibbs
Hugh Cowan
H. Watts-Robinson
Iain Rockliffe
Iain Simons
Ian Baronofsky
Ian Hosler
Ian Lydon-James
Ian Normile
Ian Stopher
Inge Strand
Ivan Bersanetti
Ivo Zoltan Frey
Jacco van t Riet
Jacob Blichfeldt
Jacob Warren
Jaime R. Bernad
Jake Gordon
Jakob Kjøller
Jakub Tyszko
James Bicknell
James Hare
James Monkman
James Lockey
James Reid
James Thomson
James Wilkinson
Jamie Battison
Jamie Holyoake
Jamie Howard
Jamie Jones
Jan-Erik Sundh
Jani Suhonen
Jan Karremans
Janne Alapeteri
Janne Suur-Näkki
Jan-Ove Lorenzen
Jarkko Lehtola
Jarle Berntsen
Jason Brown
Jason Edmunds
Jason Kunkel
Jason Micari
Jason New
Jason Perkins
Jason Robertson
Jason Timmons
Jassim Harethi
Jay Loring
Jeff Cotterman
Jeffrey Gietz
Jeffrey Pacitto
Jens Andersen
Jens Wilmer
Jeremy Chippett
Jeremy Stockman
Jeroen de Beer
Jeroen Knoester
Jerry Bonner
Jesper Brännmark
Jesse Rivera
Jessica Bex
Jim Barat
Jim Lesko
Jimmy Petersson
Joakim L. Gilje
Job Geheniau
Jochen Lämmel
Joel Stocker
Joerg Droege
Joeri ML van Haren
Jörn Kierstein
Joe Trigg
Johan Bentzen
John Allen
John Blythe
John B. Træholt
John C. Lonningdal
John Harper
John Mcshane
John Moody
John S. Eddie
John Stanley
Jonas Månsson
Jonathan Bentley
Jonathan Leung
Jonathan Quilter
Jonathan Schmidt
Jonathan Zimmitti
Jon Austwick
Jonno Downes
Jon Petersson
Jon Provencher
Jon Ward
Joona Palaste
Jordi Escobar Bonet
Jorge Cabrera
Jörg Sonntag
Jörg Weese
Josef Söntgen
Jose Luis Equiza
Josh Washburne
Jouni Smed
Jouni Vepsäläinen
Juan Fernandez
Juan Gabriel
Juha Aalto
Juha Alaniemi
Julian Harris
Julien Wyart
Jungsberger Gerhard
Jussi Ronkainen
Justin Baldock
Justin Emlay
Just Mail Team
Kai Groshert
Karen Collins
Kari-Pekka Koljonen
Karl-Johan Nilsson
Karl Todd
Kay Failla
Keaton S
Keith Day
Keith Geoghegan
Ken Barnes
Kenneth Aastrøm
Kenny Nilsson
Kevin Crate
Kevin Harris
Kevin Savetz
Kevin Tilley
Klemens Franz
Knut Kraushaar
Kolja Sennack
Komputer for alle
Krzysztof Kondrak
Kurt Klemm
Kyle Oedewaldt
L. Appleton-Webster
Larry Anderson
Lars Becker
Lars Klaeboe
Lars Kohlhardt
Lars Steinbach
Lars Willemsen
Lasse Hynninen
Laszlo Benyi
Laura Menendez
Laurent Chevrier
Leanna Conradson
Lee Cooke
Lee Evans
Lee Heise
Lee Huggett
Leif Ebeling
Leif Langsdorf
Leo de Blaauw
Leonard Pitre
Les Ellis
Lewis Lane
Liam Piesley
Lorenzo Maini
Lothar Lattermann
Louis Frederick
Luca Argentiero
Luca Ceccarelli
Luigi Rosso
Luigi Vicari
Luis Gilabert Almagro
Luke Orphanides
Luke Pinner
Lutz Dornbusch
Lutz Ohl
Maarten Sander
Mads Orbesen Troest
Maik Karbon
Maik Merten
Manuel Beckmann
Manuel S. de Diego
Marc Bell
Marc Bright
Marc Fouquet
Marcin Segit
Marc Monticelli
Marc Oberhaeuser
Marco Bonadonna
Marco Fritz
Marcus Evans
Marcus Gerards
Marcus Gullarberg
Marcus V. G. Chiado
Marc Weber
Marie-Andrée Poisson
Mario Caruffo
Mario Olivan Tenorio
Mark Buffone
Mark Cassam
Mark Guttenbrunner
Mark Hardisty
Marko Rukonic
Mark Paterson
Mark Semczyszyn
Mark Sztainbok
Mark Turner
Mark Turner
Markus Müller
Markus Sillanpää
Martijn Bosschaart
Martijn van Rheenen
Martin Bitschnau
Martin Bull
Martin Debes
Martin Grundy
Martin King
Martin Parris
Martin Riedl
Martin Schemitsch
Martin Williams
Martyn Hodgetts
Massimo Perasso
Mat Allen
Mat Gould
Mathew Inkson
Mathias Peters
Mathieu Burgerhout
Matt Allen
Matt Dainty
Matteo Serritiello
Matt Ferguson
Matthew Allen
Matthew Cannon
Matthew Deeprose
Matthew Diggens
Matthew Grimm
Matthew Kenyon
Matthew Roberts
Matthew Stringer
Matthew Wilsher
Matthias Ehinger
Matthias Thomas
Matthias Wissnet
Mattias Palsson
Mattias Wahlberg
Matt Rumble
Maxwell Neely-Cohen
Mevlut Dinc
Michael Cook
Michael Fincham
Michael Gibson
Michael Hay
Michael Heitzer
Michael Howard
Michael Kalmar
Michael Keith
Michael Keller
Michael König
Michael Lirko
Michael Lünzer
Michael Mulhern
Michael Plate
Michael P. Welch
Michael Rau
Michael Schiesewitz
Michael Stift
Michael Tedder
Michael Wojcikiewicz
Michal Ursiny
Michał Wojciechowski
Mikael Sjöberg
Mika Myllyvaara
Mike Bradford
Mike Lonesky
Mike Mika
Mike Ryan
Mike Wilcox
Mikey McCorry

Cont.

Milos Jovanovic
Murray Wallace
Narayana Venkatesh
Nathanael Nunes
Nathan Lansdell
Nathan Tannenbaum
Neal Wakenshaw
Neil Brown
Neil DeStefano
Neil Kendall
Neil Woodyatt
Nic Cusworth
Nicholas Clark
Nick Kimberley
Nick Lauritzen
Nick Sakellariou
Nicolas Clement
Nicolas Guerra
Niels Daalhuizen
Nigel Critten
Nikolaos Karypidis
N. Llewellyn-Jones
Noel Pritchard
Oddleif Torvik
Oliver Ainger
Oliver Boerner
Oliver Hermanni
Oliver Knagge
Oliver Lindau
Oliver Matzke
Oliver Schwald
Oliver Sons
Olivier Martin
Olivier Vigneresse
Oskar Smith
Owen Davies
Owen Johnson
Øyvind Lien
P-a Bäckström
Palle Johansen
Pasi Ylinen
Patrick Gerdes
Patrick Prins
Patrick Probst
Paula Norris
Paul Bracken
Paul Davies
Paul Driscoll
Paul Elstub
Paul Georgiou
Paul Hughes
Paul Kitching
Paul Knights
Paul Maskelyne
Paul Massey
Paul Monaghan
Paul Morrison
Paul Shaddock
Paul Stedman
Paul Taylor
Paul Whelan
Per Lindén
Per Martin Iversen
Pete Plank
Peter Cooper
Peter Flynn
Peter Kamp
Peter Landers
Peter Lichtmayer
Peter Mattsson
Peter Saunderson
Peter Schiffer
Peter Simon
Peter Stratford
Petr Andel
Petri Maaninka
Petri Pyy
Phil Cave
Philip B Heinemeier
Philip Morris
Philip Oliver
Pierre Arnaud
Pimoroni Ltd
Predrag Jovanovic
Ralf Griewel
Ralf Hermesdorf
Ralf Schwate
Ralph Egas
Randy Padawer
Raphael Bock
Ravi Verma
Rebecca Deeth
Remi Arnaud
Renee Jessen
René Thomsen
Rex Dylan van Coller
Rhys Wynne
Richard Beckett
Richard Davey
Richard Gale
Richard Heath
Richard Jefferies
Richard Jones
Richard Trenberth
Richard Wilks
Rick Haberhauer
Rick Klaassen
Rienk Harkema
Risnoddlas Grytarbiff
Robbin Tapper
Robbin van Ooij
Rob Clayton
Rob Crowther
Rob Caporetto
Robert Carrico
Robert Engel
Roberto
Roberto Mascia
Robert Shoemate
Robert Stanco
Robert Troughton
Robert Walker
Rob Hewson
Robin Deitch
Robin Ellis
Rocco Di Leo
Roel Nieskens
Roland Evers
Rowan Crawford
Roy Fielding
Roy Strickson
Rudi van der Heide
Rune L Meland
Rune Præst
Rune Vendler
Ryan Oliver
Ryan Omar
Sally Moore
Sami Inkinen
Sami Saarela
Samuel Berguerand
Samuel Gardener
Samuel Russell
Santhosh Nairstone
Sascha Engmann
Sascha Glade
Sascha Goto
Sascha Stolingwa
Scott Davies
Scott Liddell
Séamus Hoban
Sean Johnson
Sean Smith
Sebastian Bachmann
Sebastian Bober
Sebastian Skarupke
Sergio Pennacchini
Shahid Naqwi
Shane Williams
Shaun Stephenson
Sicco de Vries
Silvio Krvaric
Simone Tagliaferri
Simon Finn
Simon Hadlington
Simon Hardy
Simon Newsham
Simon Landureau
Simon Peter Hughes
Simon Peterson
Simon Shirley
Simon Stokes
Simon Stott
Smudger07
Søren Niedziella
S. Stelling-de San Antonio
Steen Larsen
Stefan Berghuis
Stefano Canali
Stefano Pasotti
Stefan Pitsch
Stefan Uhlmann
Stefan Winterstein
Stein Pedersen
Stelios Kalogreades
Stephan Guenther
Stephan Junker
Stephan Ricken
Stephen Bruce
Stephen Elkins
Stephen Hilliard
Stephen Holland
Stephen Kitt
Stephen Melville
Stephen Norman
Stephen Orr
Stephen Preston
Stephen Swan
Steve De George
Steve Erickson
Steve Mcgillivray
Steven Bodey
Steven Dalton
Steven Emery
Steven McGarr
Stian Bjelvin Schultz
Stuart Gould
Stuart McVicar
Stuart Walton
Scott Peter Wilson
Stuart Wilson
Suginami-ku
Sukhpal Singh
Sylvain Swimer
Tamas Bako
Tate Arbon
Taylor Woll
Teodor Bjerrang
Terje Høiback
Tero Lindeman
Terry Greer
Thomas Berger
Thomas Biedorf
Thomas Boecker
Thomas Frauenknecht
Thomas Porsborn
Thomas Touzimsky
Thomas Wirtzmann
Thomas Zill
Thom Moesker
Thorsten Kaufmann
Tim Ashton
Tim Fothergill
Tim Kane
Tim Koch
Tim Lapetino
Timo Dunkel
Timothy Johnson
Tim Vüllers
Tim Wheatley
Tobias Broljung
Tobias Göhlke
Tobias Hultman
Tobias Lampert
Tobias Lundmark
Tomasz Walasik
Tomi Kokki
Tomi Liiten
Tommaso Teruzzi
Tommes Koch
Tommi Lempinen
Tom Offringa
Tom Phillips
Tom Vergult
Toni Martin Villalta
Tony Cruise
Torben Harms
Torben Weide
Tordbjørn W. Eriksen
Torsten Gunst
Torsten Linnenbrink
Trevor Briscoe
Trevor Storey
Troy Benjamin
Troy Lonergan
Truls Osmundsen
Tuomas Halonen
Tyler Sigman
Vanja Utne
Veronese Alessio
Victor Pedersen
Ville Peltola
Vincenzo Mainolfi
Vizzacchero Sebastien
Warren Lapworth
Wayne Keenan
Werner Rott
Widar B. Rødder
William Lane
William Prince
Will Morton
Xavier Bodenand
Yann Barthelemy
Yannick Suter
YrJö Hämäläinen
Yves Bolognini
Zack Scott
Zsolt Gáspár

Hi, my name is Rocco Di Leo and I run dustlayer.com, a blog about coding the Commodore C64. If you are curious about how people created cool stuff in the old times and how enthusiasts still do today, feel free to stop by.

Connect via actraiser@dustlayer.com or @actraiser on Twitter.

Beach-Head loader / 1983 / Access Software